Turning The
PAGES

HOW EXPLORING MY PAST LIVES LED ME ON THE
JOURNEY OF HEALING MEMORIES, AND WHAT I
LEARNED WHILE TRAVELING BACK IN TIME

ALLA KALUZHNY

BALBOA.PRESS
A DIVISION OF HAY HOUSE

"Alla's debut book demonstrates how important it is to hold the vision of a dream and allow it to unfold in our physical reality. She shares her own personal stories of her past lives, creating a compelling collection of stories to inspire and expand the reader."

—Christy Whitman,
New York Times bestselling author

"Reading this book will open your eyes, mind, and especially your heart to your soul's journey through time, enrich your inner world, and let your imagination soar to yet unknown places."

—Christina Hill,
2-time presenter Carnegie Hall NYC & world-renowned channeler for Athella

'Turning The Pages' is not just another testimonial for reincarnation but a manifestation of a lifelong spiritual journey of self-discovery; it is the result of the courage and burning desire to travel treacherous paths in search of answers to life's most painful and personal questions.

—Lana Kirtser
Astrologer, IT Consultant, Family Friend

CONTENTS

THE WORD TO MY READER

This book is about my past lives, my convictions, and my belief in reincarnation. It's a story of my Soul's many journeys woven together and lived in different bodies, different historical times, and different countries. Uncovering and then writing about these lives brought together my spiritual quest, the deeply-held belief that we have more than one life to live, my ongoing desire to heal physical challenges, and my firm intention to become healthy. Each story in this book is about a different incarnation and connection I found between then and now.

Discovering my past lives turned out to be educational, inspirational, uplifting, and even life-affirming for me. It confirmed that it's more to us than just the physical body and sparked my curiosity to educate myself about reincarnation. It inspired and encouraged me to know myself better and search for many ways to become my own healer. Although the book is about life, death, and dying, it instilled faith and hope that the Soul is timeless and will continue its journey. This writing experience empowered and expanded my awareness and gave me a new sense of confidence in my skills and a newly founded gratitude for my life-long education in Spiritual Psychology.

I hope this book will become a starting point for your personal journey and an exploration into your prior lives and inspire and lead to your spiritual growth and expansion. By the time you finish reading this book, the following shifts may occur:

- You start questioning whether you might have had past lives and have been on this planet before;
- You may start seeing your relationships with family, friends, co-workers in a different way and wondering if you met them or knew them from another time,
- Your interest in past lives may cause you to become more observant, mindful, aware, and awake.
- You may start entertaining the idea that You are not a Human Being having a Spiritual Experience, but You Are a Spiritual Being having a Human Experience.
- You notice that reading about past lives may have a healing effect on you and help you release some old memories and emotions.

and what this dream could mean. Sometimes I asked friends experienced in dreamwork, telling them about that unusual dream and especially the stuck-together pages because I wanted to know the answer. My friends usually gave me similar explanations, saying that I could not open the pages and see the pictures because I was consciously not ready to see them yet. They said that my subconscious mind was protecting me from something I yet would not understand or process. YET was a keyword. Many times, over the years, these words proved to be true.

Over time, different lifetimes came to my awareness under various circumstances: sometimes in meditation or during a regression session. Other times a sensory image or a vision came to me while visiting a random place. I believed that what I saw in my mind or knew on the gut level was real because I felt them physically, emotionally, and mentally.

I was always intrigued by unusual, mystical, not logically explainable things, and I wanted to learn about them as much as possible.

I remembered in the 90s watching the daily show 'The Other Side' and my state of shock when I heard for the first time the words, "We are not Humans having Spiritual experience; We Are Spirits having Human Experience." I felt unexplainable excitement and the recognition that it was true. I Am Spirit having a human experience. That statement was revolutionary and immediately shifted my perception, instantly placing me on the journey of learning about myself, where I came from, and my purpose.

After that awareness, I wanted to immerse myself in spiritual studies, and this desire led me to USM (the University of Santa Monica), the Master's Program in Spiritual Psychology. The school's curriculum was just what I desired to learn, and I knew without a doubt that I was "guided" there by my Intuition. The studies at USM prompted spiritual growth, expanded my conscious awareness and spiritual awakening, bringing forward many forgotten memories.

One of the memories was that dream about the book with the pages stuck together. Oh, those pages! Like a mysterious whisper, they were calling on me, luring me to search for clues. I thought of the images I remembered and the pictures I did not remember, but of course, most of all, I thought about those stuck-together pages and the meaning behind them. Thinking about past lives made me wonder about graves, the graves where "my" bodies were laid to rest. And I thought of how intriguing it would be to find graves of my past lives, see the headstones and find out who I was.

Growing up, I was curious about past existences without really knowing what it meant. I also remember that growing up I often felt tired and wanted to nap or rest. When I was about ten years old, coming home from school and feeling tired, the thought crossed my mind: "I wonder who I was in my last life, that I am so tired in this one?" The answer was instant. The quiet voice inside uttered, "a prostitute. You worked hard and died young."

I brushed off the answer because, frankly, I didn't even know the meaning of that word, yet I accepted it and memorized it. It was not the word I heard before in my childhood, especially growing up in the Soviet Union and being ten years old. When I grew older and learned its meaning, I felt deep shame and embarrassment associated with someone so unworthy. Yet, my recurrent fatigue was a reminder of a little girl's query into chronic tiredness. Curiously, I was not interested in finding out more and preferred not to give any credence to it.

Until I came to the US from the former Soviet Union, I never read any books on reincarnation, and except for my childhood memory, I did not have any other frame of reference. My first introduction to this topic happened in the early 90s when I saw a random talk show with Dr. Brian Weiss. He was promoting his new book *Through Time into Healing*. Everything he said in his presentation gave me a jolt of energy (the goosebumps); it was an awakening on the cellular level, and I was mesmerized by what he was saying and sharing with his audience. Of course, I bought the book (there was no Amazon yet) and read it in an instance.

The idea and desire to write my book were often popping up in my mind, and this desire was fueled by other people asking me whether I had written a book. I could write about plenty of topics, but all the ideas were short-lived and did not have an appeal or a passion for taking them seriously.

One day, during my yoga class's meditation, an idea about the future book, its name, and even how to construct it -all came at once. In my mind, I saw a blue book named Alla's Past Lives, printed in yellow diagonally across the cover. The book that I saw in meditation reminded me of the one dream from over 20 years ago, a dream I had before my 40th birthday but have not forgotten. This idea did not come as a big surprise because, since that famous dream, I had uncovered over at least a dozen lifetimes. When my Intuition during the meditation showed me the book's working title and an idea of how to organize it, I was grateful for the Divine Guidance and the information I intuitively received.

I envision that the process of writing this book will be like visiting those gravesites. Still, it will be more therapeutic, healing, and transformational on all four levels of my being. I remembered the feeling when this idea came to me. It felt like an old, murky window inside of me was suddenly opened wide, and fresh air entered my Soul, letting the stale energy out. Even more, the sense of freedom came over me, and I felt a great deal of enthusiasm. The incredible opportunity to learn about myself, peek into the mystery of my past existences, and find out what might have happened to my Soul over many lives was very thrilling and inspiring. I wanted to find answers to my questions about myself, my certain behaviors and triggers, relationships, likes and dislikes, life choices, and so many other things. I was ready to step into unknown territory and let the healing of awakening begin.

And this is how it all began.

CHAPTER 1

"Some people believe that we go on living in another body after death, that we lived before. They call it reincarnation. That we all lived before on the earth thousands of years ago or on some other planet. They say we have forgotten it. Some say they remember their past lives."
—James Joyce

Solid like a Rock

As you just read, on the very first page of the book from a long-ago dream of past lives, was a picture of a boulder, a huge rock lying under the sun. Seeing this picture in my mind brings me a sense of serenity, positive energy, and maybe even a smile. I believe this Rock was my first incarnation on this planet as my soul chose an inanimate object to adjust to this new mysterious planet and be. I think it was wise to learn, observe, and experience the life my soul had chosen to become a boulder, a rock. The Rock does not change; it's stable, reliable, and solid. When I think about these qualities, the words "Solid Like a Rock" come to mind. My first incarnation seemed to add to the merits of my future lives, future lives' experiences, and future events and circumstances.

Like a Rock, I was just there. New life was waking up around, under, and above me. The Rock was a non-threatening entity that no one paid attention to and overlooked. I saw strange creatures that were passing by in groups or alone. When the sun was going down, I would leave the Rock and fly away, travel back to my home planet to visit my kin and share with them about that strange planet I now was a part of. My home planet did not have sunsets and sunrises, the light was always there, and it was so different and unusual to feel the coldness in the Rock as the sun was setting. When it felt too cold to the Rock, the soul looked for adventures flying around the universe. Many of my kin mates were like me, planting their souls in the earthly objects, getting to know the place, and some birthed into the creatures that lived there before we started exploring this magnificent planet. I found my location close to the water, and it was a prime location!

I saw creatures with or without fur; four, six, and eight-legged beings. I saw two-legged creatures that jumped from trees; I saw enormous flying beasts. Some were resting next to me, hiding in the shade that I projected. I loved to welcome different critters; then, I could see them better, smell them, and understand them more. I was always curious to observe how these beings resting under me were interacting with each other. Those that came by two soon came with miniature copies of themselves, and these creatures tend to be protective over the mini-versions of the big ones. Sometimes I saw creatures scuffling and hurting each other, but I could not comprehend why. On my home planet, we lived in total harmony, we were sincere in caring for each other and every one of us, and we comforted each other if they requested it. We sent signals to all, and all were sending comforting messages back for support and care.

My travels to this new planet began one day when we received a call for volunteers for a critical assignment from our higher-level teachers that a planet in the Multiverse needs to up-level of consciousnesses. Those who agreed to explore and help a new planet were warned that despite unimaginable beauty, pristine nature, and changes in darkness and light times that happen simultaneously in different parts of this mysterious planet, multiple dangers and challenges were lurking everywhere. We were forewarned to be alert, ready, and focused at all times. It was impressed upon us that creatures that lived on this planet were so dense and hard to penetrate that it would take several millennia to make a dent in the collective consciousness and up-level it. The teachers cautioned us that when we start living amongst them, we will become like them, be them. They said we could only come back and stay and rest on our mother planet when we swap one body for another. However, we expected to return to the beautiful blue planet in a new, dense body.

Our planet's high gurus wanted our mission to be a complete success, and they met with us one on one telling us that though they could not foresee all that might happen on the blue planet at different times, they promised that we could go home and rest and visit while we were changing bodies. That promise of going back home from time to time and rest was so reassuring and comforting that I and many of my kin agreed to this challenge and signed up to become first explorers. One of my kin asked how many bodies we had to change to complete this assignment; however, there was no firm answer. Moreover, one of our high-level guides said he anticipated that we would forget about our home planet once engaged in this assignment. We will continue to play roles, only remembering our home when a body we lived in would be ready to be shed. He said that we would not remember any of what he was saying to us now, and at times will experience a state of regret (he called it a feeling of sadness) for a body we just left. He challenged us with every thought he was signaling to us, but we became more determined and ready to take on this assignment.

We all agreed and communicated the same thought: AS LONG AS WE CAN SOMETIMES RETURN HOME, REST, VISIT OUR KIN, and EACH OTHER, WE WANT TO HELP THE PLANET TO UPGRADE ITS CONSCIOUSNESS. It was impressed upon us that it will take many different bodies and events to see a shift on the planet. Many refinements and personal evolutions of the body and brain indicate the rise of awareness, up-leveling, and growth in consciousness. They told us to be on alert, that once we observe and notice such a change in a personal shift in consciousness, we were to protect, support, and expand it and carry it on to the next body. We agreed to all conditions and, like fireflies, were prepared to be transported to a planet that attracted our imagination and stirred up a state of celebration (feeling excitement). It was made known to us that beings from other planets headed to this blue planet as well. Still, their assignments differed from ours; we were to up-level, up-lift, up-grade; but the others' missions were not so noble and had more sinister plans for the blue planet. They wanted to enslave the inhabitants of the blue planet, make them inferior, seed negativity, hostility, competition, distrust, and division among them. Our teachers warned us about possible confrontations, animosity between other occupants and us, and sometimes even wars. Our group was firm in their convictions, and without any more delays, we went.

Everything happened as our elders cautioned us about, and even more unpredictable, dangerous adventures waited for us to face and situations to mend. We were up to a challenge, and with our every return to a new body, our precious memories of the home planet were fading away for some less, for some more. Yet, we continued coming back, embodying qualities of the planet's inhabitants and striving to live up to our promise to awaken the earth and raise its consciousness. And we are still here, on this blue planet, fighting and carrying on.

CHAPTER 2

"The Warrior remembers the past"
—Paulo Coelho

The Destiny of the Warrior

The next page from the book my husband gifted me in that prophetic dream depicted a brutal battle of warriors dressed in armor, with swords and shields. The image of that battle was in the dark forest, and it was either early morning or an early evening because it seemed dimmed on the picture in my dream. Who was I fighting against, where was I from, and who was I?

Two things were for certain: I was a man, strong, tall, young, and powerful. I was fighting to protect what was dear to me and those on my side.

"I belonged to a royal family and was called to war that lasted years, even before I was born into the royal family. My mother was our Queen's cousin, and my playmates were many other children belonging to the royal family. My father was in the army and was already fighting this war against our enemy. This war was between England and France; it was 1467 when I was born. Ever since I remembered myself, I remembered my father returning to the palace from the battle, tired but glad to be alive. He would lift me in the air, holding me tight in his strong arms and telling me: "you are going to be this tall, you are going to be so strong, and you will take my place when you grow older. I am counting on you to be brave, fair, and good to your warriors; you will be trusted with their lives when you are old enough to step up and lead your warriors to battles. Your victories will depend on your soldiers and your knowing them and caring for them well.

These words have etched in my memory, and when I was old enough, I was given a small sword as a gift and trained to fight. I knew to better live up to the expectations of my loving father, who saw me as his extension, his legacy, and his pride. I was taught to follow in his footsteps and learn his art as a warrior, protector, and loyal countryman that served his King and Queen. My name was Paul, and my mother, who was our Queen's cousin, was loving but firm with me, and she never prevented my father from raising me in strict and harsh ways. She watched and agreed when he encouraged my competitive side to open and grow and pushed me to become who I was not: stern, firm, and militaristic.

His task was to make me as aggressive as he wanted me to be because he saw my gentle nature and knew that I would not survive to be a dreamer and a softy. My father talked to me from the time I was little, explaining why his parenting was so unkind at times. He wanted me to know how much he loved me, yet, he wanted me to be strong and courageous and live life as a warrior. And this is who I became, from a dreamer and a poet to a warrior. But inside, I was dying every time I had to kill an enemy in the battle. I was dying inside when, on the battlefield, my loyal men were mercilessly killed, and I could not protect them. I was dying inside every time I saw my horses die on the battlefield.

Blood, destruction, and death were my constant companions when I was on the battlefield. When I came to my palace and saw my mother's eyes filled with love and fear for me and my life, I decided against having any children. I could not bring a child onto this scary world and be frightened about his fate. It was a great fortune that my father survived all the battles and was only wounded. I don't know my fate, but I can be sent to heaven any day, judging from what surrounds me. I could not bear the thought of having my own family and then being killed, leaving them to mend on their own. I presumed it was selfish of me, but the choice was made long ago because I grew up seeing my poor mother crying her eyes out every time my father left for battle; I still feel sadness remembering that her hugs were especially tender when my father was gone for many months.

I think both of my parents understood my choice and quietly gave me their support. When I was 28, I returned to the battlefield after a short visit home. I spent time with my buddies, I had a fling with one beautiful woman, but knowing my limits, I never promised myself or her love life. My duty was to serve our Queen, and I never forgot my oath.

Unfortunately, upon my return to the battlefield, my army was treacherously attacked by the enemy in the early hours of dawn. We could barely collect our armor, by then many men were viciously killed. I was fighting with all my might with two enemies, not seeing that the real danger was behind me. My shield did not protect my back, and the very last thing I remembered was the excruciating pain in my spine from a heavy sword that broke my back. My life ended on the battlefield in that predawn hour. I thought I was ready to face death, but it came behind my back."

When Paul stopped telling his story, I immediately compared the deadly injury to his spine and subsequent death with my current life's injury to my spine. I recognized the same pattern of "knife in the back" as a theme of betrayal I experienced many times in life. Some betrayals were small, some big, and some left gushing wounds because they came from the back like any betrayal. Unlike Paul, I did not die physically, but with each betrayal, something inside me died every time when my back was taking another invisible wound, and my heart was left broken. Over the years, I accepted that betrayals are a big part of our human experience. They are part of our psychological makeup, and we all play the game of betrayal to ourselves and others. Betrayals leave us with wounds, physical and emotional, and we all are trying to heal them, doing the best we can.

And So It Is.

CHAPTER 3

"Traveling to past lives is like making a hole in the floor and letting the flames of the fire in the apartment below scorch and burn the present."
— **Paulo Coelho**

Burning the Witch

This lifetime did not come from my dream book, or maybe it did, but it was on one of the pages I could not open. The way it revealed itself was unforgettable and happened one sunny day in August of 2003, right before my graduation from USM. I was in Palm Springs with my graduating class at Practicum, culminating in our 2-year Spiritual Psychology program. We spent five days in the desert, and it was very transformational, in essence, healing five days.

Every morning we gathered for class, and each class started with a 20 minutes meditation. I was looking forward to this process, knowing the healing power of almost two hundred people meditating in one room at the same time. On the third day of our program, I was eager to start the meditation because I thought of a question, I wanted to know the answer to. I wanted to know about the spiritual (third) eye and why it did not work the way I wanted it to work. Throughout my second year of studies at USM, I was trying to "wake it up," but it stubbornly refused to cooperate, and I wanted to know why; I was determined to get an answer that morning.

When the meditation began, I inwardly asked why my spiritual eye was asleep. In complete silence, I suddenly heard the answer in my head: "Because I need to protect you." "Protect from what?' -I asked. "Protect from harm" was the answer. 'I am safe here; what could happen to me?" I continued the dialogue. The answer came to me in the most unexpected, frightening way. I started feeling my feet becoming very hot at that moment, and the heat was quickly moving up my legs. I felt as if I was engulfed in flames, that I was burning, and then I knew I was not alone.

I "saw" other women engulfed in flames next to me. We all were tied to a big pile of dry branches, and our screams from pain and horror were reaching the sky. What have we done, what did I do to deserve this terrible death? I asked, panicking. Everything that was happening to me was so real and scary that I even stopped breathing from fear. Who was I, and what caused my excruciating end? Who did it to me?

At that moment in my mind's eyes, I saw a man wearing a cape. He was in the crowd of people who were watching and cheering the burning. I instantly knew he was there to confirm my peril. I looked at his eyes as I was screaming from pain and anguish; our eyes locked, and he rapidly walked away from the crowd and me. When I asked my Higher Self what I did to him, why he wanted to harm me, the voice said that he came to me for advice, and I told him the truth. That angered him, and he sent me to death as a witch.

The advice I gave him came from reading Tarot Cards, and because I was a prolific card reader and told him what I saw, he, out of revenge, killed me. This vision happened within seconds, but the burning sensation and the gripping fear stayed in my body.

When these memories flooded my consciousness, I understood why activating my third eye was such a challenge. Though I desired to develop my clairvoyant abilities, something was preventing me from it. This something was protecting me from putting myself in harm's way. It was the sole reason I could not tell a story looking at the cards, no matter how long I studied and knew them well; I could not do a coherent reading as if some higher power prevented me. I remember how the physical sensation of heat was moving quickly up my body and how terrifying the feeling was. It was my very first time painfully reliving my death in such a tragic way.

I could not wait for the meditation to be over so that I could tell Ron and Mary (our professors and USM teachers) what just happened. I did not usually share in the large group; however, this time I almost jumped out of my seat, raising my hand to be called to share. When I was called to share, I could barely hold my tears and emotions back. Yet, Ron did not seem to be amused at all. He was nodding his head in the validation of my retelling of what I just experienced. He said that many of us (the students in the class) had been persecuted, experienced violent deaths in prior existences; there were reasons why in this life, many of us were hesitant or afraid to speak up, to stand up in fears of physical harm and even death. Ron's explanation and calm demeanor helped me to calm down and overcome the shaking and the terror I was still feeling in my body and heart.

With time I realized that this terrifying glimpse into the distant past was a key for opening up many other lives because, after this unprovoked memory download, I knew I was here before. That episode was very traumatic and unforgettable on both physical and emotional levels. I kept processing this memory of life as a witch. But I was not a witch. I was a beautiful young woman with dark hair, piercing eyes, a very melodic voice, an infectious laugh, and a kind smile. I had friends; I had a family. I was not alone. I loved animals that lived on the streets and fed them whatever I could. I knew that the gift of clairvoyance and predictions came through my paternal grandmother Lucille. Unfortunately, my parents died early, leaving my younger sister Kerry and me alone until my grandmother stepped in to take us in, to care for us, and raise us.

My grandmother lived in a large quarter and even had servants. She knew and practiced "The Craft," but she also knew how unsafe it was. She had to hide her knowledge and her craft from everyone. I did not know what she was doing until I walked on her looking at the large crystal sphere in the middle of the hidden room. She was saying words in a language I did not understand. The room was filled with candles big and small; the smoke was coming out of the big pot filled with shimmering water placed in the corner of the room. This smoke was changing colors, and I became utterly captivated by this unusual scene. I noticed that the smoke changed colors and created different shapes, and these magical formations, floating on their own, continued to sparkle and move like in a dance.

I was mesmerized by the scene and did not pay attention to my grandmother walking toward me. She was not upset; she was not angry. She put her arms around me and gently laughed, enjoying my stupor. She then said that I was not supposed to be in this room and walked me out, closing the door tightly. Ever since this moment in my life (I was about 15), I could not think of anything but those shapes, magical, colorful shapes, floating in the room and above the boiling pot. I saw them in my dreams, I saw them during the day, and they were everywhere I looked, calling on me, inviting me, surrounding me. Once I asked my little sister if she saw anything around her, but she said she did not see anything. I saw them sometimes less, sometimes more, yet always there.

I started asking my grandmother to let me in the secret room, but she did not let me in, saying that it was not for me, that I would be better off not ever stepping into this hidden room again. I loved and respected my grandmother, who gave my sister and me home and cared for us, and I wanted to obey her and her request not to go to that mysterious room. For a while, I did withstand the urges to peek in the room again. However, one morning I was looking for my grandmother, and though I was unsure where to find her, I followed my intuition that led me to her.

Once again, I pushed that door, and now, knowing what to anticipate, I saw the whole room filled with moving radiant shapes that were dancing with each other, twisting, swarming, playing, and calling my name that I heard in my head. My grandmother was standing above the crystal sphere and watched the images appearing there. I came closer to see what she saw when she turned her head, looking at me without her usual warm smile.

She gave me a long look and told me sternly that I have a choice. The choice between a good life as a married woman with children or as a castaway. I could learn her craft, but then I would have to leave her home and be on my own, living among simple people and earning money. Because of my age, I was almost ready to be married into a distinguished family. She warned me of the dangers, betrayals surrounding this lonely way of life and told me to think over and choose wisely. My loving grandmother was dead serious, even stern, and I felt that she meant it.

I quietly left the room and hid in my corner. I covered my head with a blanket and stayed there for a long time. I was to decide my fate for the rest of my life at this moment. I could stay here; she would find me a fine noble young man, and we would get engaged, married. I would become a respected woman with children, servants, and life that would be predictable, maybe mundane at times. However, my grandmother wanted and wished for this life for me. Yet, the other choice was so appealing, romantic, and adventurous, so creative and dangerous at the same time. I felt that I did not have a choice. The iridescent shapes appeared around me and seductively started dancing before my eyes once again. As they were calling me, I heard voices: come, come with us. I fell asleep, and the shapes continued to dance in my dream. I could not shake them off, even if I wanted to. When I woke up, I came to my grandmother, telling her everything I thought, experienced, and felt since she sent me away to think. I described to her the radiant shapes I've been seeing around me, calling my name. She smiled at me. But her smile was not a happy and usual warm smile: it was more of a forced smile. My grandmother reluctantly succumbed to my decision.

From that time on, I was allowed very quietly, almost unnoticeably in the hidden room and just observe my grandmother's actions and creations. I was mesmerized by everything she was doing, demonstrating, and teaching me. I agreed with her- under no circumstances could I tell my younger sister Kerry what I was doing and learning from my grandmother. At the same time, my sister and I continued our studies at home, as we had the teacher coming every day and giving us lessons in reading and history. We then had to learn and present the next day. My sister and I both adored our teacher, who was strict, nurturing, and kind. My grandmother paid him well to educate us; she wanted to give us everything she possibly could, and thanks to God, she had the means to do so. My sister was excellent in arithmetic, I liked to read and write, and we both were good students, excelling in our studies.

I was bound by the agreement not to give my sister a hint of what I was doing, but as she got older, it was becoming harder. She was curious, sometimes asking me where I was when she wanted to play with me.

Three years passed by quickly, and during this time, I was learning the craft that my grandmother was showing me, not as much teaching and explaining. I studied the magical cards, and I felt electricity coming through my body every time I held them. My ability to see things that were not physically there (like colorful shapes from the boiling pot) increased and I could hear sounds and know things ahead of time.

I knew the danger of insisting on living on my own among people who could potentially hurt me. I heard stories of women and men who practiced the same craft and were persecuted in the most terrible ways, and as I grew older, the sense of reality became more evident.

I knew that my grandmother continued wishing for me to decide otherwise, that I would stay with her, marry, and have a family, becoming a noble, respectable woman. I knew how desperate she was at times because I would catch her look full of sadness. But my calling was stronger than the love and respect I had for my grandmother, and one day I knew it was time.

I told my grandmother that I was ready and saw tears in her eyes. I got my few belongings together and my grandmother gave me some money to start my independent living. She asked me to go to a nearby town, not to stay here. I hugged my sister, who was unaware of my leaving, and she cried and cried. Separating from Kerry was difficult; separating from my grandmother was difficult; leaving my room, my books, the roof over my head, and my feeling of safety and security were difficult. The night before I decided to leave, I had a dream where both of my parents came to me. They hugged me and told me they loved me and always will be by my side, but they wouldn't be able to protect me from harm, only warn. They said they wanted me to have a long life, a good life, a life where I can be cared for and respected, and they wanted me to rethink my decision to be on my own.

They disappeared without waiting for my answer, and I woke up. I did not share this dream with my grandmother; I did not want to add more pain. Despite all the warnings, I left my home. I had to dress down, not to attract bad people to me. I walked to another nearby town and came to a center, looking around, deciding what to do next. Two women that happened to be sisters came by and asked if I needed help. I said I was looking for a place to stay and some work to do. They happened to be local prophets, and they needed someone to help keep their home in order. I smiled inside, thanking God for bringing me to these women and showing the way. The sisters were nice and treated me fairly. From them, I learned other skills, like mind reading, understanding the relation between sound and healing, and much more. However, the cards were my favorite. They were my friends. They were my confidants, I trusted them completely, and I played with them every day.

After staying with these women for a while, I became more familiar with the town, with people who lived around, and I was immensely thankful to my saviors, the women who were so kind and gracious toward me. One day I approached them, telling them how grateful I was to them for everything. They did not want me to leave, as I was a good helper, I was pleasant and had good relationships with other people living on the property, and I was kind to animals. But though I felt trepidation of stepping out on my own once again, out of the safety of my generous hosts' home, I knew I had to leave like I left my grandmother. I had a sense of knowing, telling me to go. While I was still working for the sisters, I found a tiny house behind which began a local forest. I walked by a few times, but no one seemed to live there. One day I knocked on the door of a nearby house with no gate, and when asked about that tiny house, I was told that people who lived there died, and since then, no one wanted to live there. It's been empty for a long time. I started going there to clean up, and the more I visited that old unoccupied, and unclaimed house, the surer I was that I could live there. The forest did not scare me; moreover, the trees quietly whispered to me to come and play with them and sit in their shade.

When I told the sisters about what I had found they wanted to see it, and they walked with me to the other side of our town to see it. They did not like the place and proximity to a forest, but they did not want to hold me back and asked me to stay with them until winter is over so that I don't freeze there by myself. They also asked me to come and live with them every winter and only be in the house when it was warm. I truly appreciated their kindness and agreed. Little did I know that I would not be alive next winter and won't take them up on their kind invitation.

When the spring came, I left the sisters and was excited to be on my own. People were familiar with me; I was one of a few mystics on this side of the town, and little by little, some neighbors started coming over to get advice. I did not take any money, but they always brought food for me, so I had plenty to feed myself and my animal friends that lived on the streets. One man came to my place several times; his interest was around money. He was tall, dressed in a black cape, with his face hidden. But he could not hide his eyes. They were cold, suspicious, distrustful, and uncaring.

I thought he was hiding his real voice too. I felt he preferred my place because it was next to a forest, and he could appear and disappear unnoticed into the night. He paid well; he was the only one who paid money for my advice and readings. I had some fears when he first started coming over, and I sensed that he could be dangerous, but after a few times, I got used to him, and because he paid, I did not want to turn him away. Every time he seemed satisfied with my advice and even warmed up to me. His eyes appeared not as cold as before, and one time I also sensed a smile. But he never told me his name, and I still felt apprehensive when he suddenly appeared at my door.

That fateful day he came more upset than I ever saw him and asked me to read cards about a certain man. When I started reading the cards, giving him the answer, he was asking for, from what I read in the cards, he became enraged, smashing the table the cards were on. He called me a liar; he said I betrayed him, and my cards were no good, and they lied the same as me. He left abruptly, and his behavior terrified me.

I did not know what to do or what to expect. I left my house and stayed in the woods to calm down. At first, I did not understand why he became so angry, but then remembered that he appeared already upset when he came in. I should have been more careful in my openness and naivety. I could not stop feeling doom and gloom, and though I tried not to feel this way, the creeping fear grasped me by the throat and the heart. I went to sleep with this feeling, having scary dreams.

Early in the morning, I was awakened by a loud knocking on my door, and when I opened the door, my heart dropped to the floor. I saw big men with pitchforks that were threatening, and they yelled: "you are a witch; you lied to our master. You will be punished for your lies, witch; you will pay." I told them that I was not a witch; I was just guiding people, but they did not want to listen to my words; they grabbed me by my hair and dragged me on the horse cart. I became quiet, knowing that screaming and crying won't help. I was taken to jail and was thrown on the floor with other young women already being there. The priest came to jail, prayed for our souls, and said that we were lost souls and were doomed to die. Then we were dragged to the center of a large town square, and when I saw large tree branches tied together, I knew my fate.

The crowd was cheering, pointing fingers at us, and some of us were crying, asking to forgive, but I was quiet; all my tears dried out. At this moment, I saw my old friends, those colorful shapes that started dancing in the ground and around me. They came back to me at the very last moments of my life to remind me that of the choices I had made when I left my grandmother's comfort and turned away the sisters' kindness brought me to this tragic end.

I felt my heart freeze when I saw cold, dark, soulless eyes piercing me. He came to witness my death. It infuriated me, and I yelled. I yelled at him and placed a curse on him for seven generations to have such an illness that no one could cure. These were my last words before I asked for forgiveness from my grandmother, my baby sister, and the sisters. The flame started taking over my body, the crowd was cheering, but our screams, pleas, and cries fell on deaf ears of this cruel, unwashed crowd who just wanted to be entertained and did not care about our lives, our pains, or our demise.

My soul slowly lifted and floated above my torched body, watching it crumble and succumbing to the flames consuming mine and other women's bodies. Women who met this tragic death with me. Their souls were floating above next to mine. We all formed a circle, watching in regret what happened to our young, beautiful bodies that were consumed by human cruelness, hatred, fears, ignorance, and their lowest desire to destroy all they could not understand or explain. When the torture, unbearable pain, and execution were finally over, I floated to say goodbye to the sisters, blessing them for all warmth, goodness, and caring they gave me. My next and the last stop was my grandmother and my baby sister. I saw them attending to their chores, my sister was all grown up, and my grandmother was still strong and well. None of them would know what happened to me and how tragically my life ended.

Shortly after, my parents greeted me; they waited for me to join them; there was no need to tell them how my life ended, as they knew it all.

CHAPTER 4

"Buddhists believe that you are who you are today is because
of who you have been in all your past lives."
— **Frederick Lenz**

The Monk

The story of this past life is not straight-forward like the ones before or after. This one has its twists and turns and, in my belief, involves a walk-in (a spirit that took over a body by agreement). It does sound too weird, I understand. Still, I want to be transparent and honest in my storytelling and heal the memory of this life.

It all began when I went to a preschool at the age of 4 1/2. My mother was pregnant with my younger brother. My parents decided that it was time for me to enter preschool, and to make it easier for me, they enrolled me at the school where my aunty was working. However, my preschool experience was short and unpleasant. I was not too fond of the place and didn't want to be there. I remember protesting napping there; I did not like to be told what to do, and being a free spirit for four years of my life, I did not want to obey and listen. So I viewed this whole experience as punishment.

My brother was born in April, and right before my 5th birthday in May, I contracted chickenpox at the preschool. My poor baby brother got infected too. I remember his tiny body covered in a green antiseptic solution that we have called "Zelenka" Zelenka is used on wounds, scrapes, and other skin conditions, for example, chickenpox bumps. I also was covered in Zelenka from head to toes, and I remember feeling itchy, miserable, and annoyed by everything. In a few days, instead of getting better, my condition worsened. The chickenpox virus attacked my brain, causing brain inflammation, violent headaches, vomiting, and meningitis.

The mundane chickenpox turned almost deadly for me in an instance. I was rushed to the hospital, and my mother had to be with me because I needed 24-hour care. So, she had to leave her newborn child to save the other one. Cruel. My condition was getting worse. The inflammation took over the part of the brain responsible for speech, and I lost any ability to speak. I became mute. For two weeks, I did not utter a word. I was making some sounds, pointing to my mother to give me something I wanted, but could not say a word. Even to this day, I remember how violently I was vomiting from the excruciating headaches. But the doctors were too afraid to move me, letting me stay in all that vomit as it was raging out of me.

I was between life and death during these days, burning with fever, and was heavily hallucinating. The doctors did not think I would make it, and as a last hope effort, they wanted my parents to consider a spinal tap to relieve brain fluid and stop the inflammation. They had to do it twice, and only after the second procedure, I started showing improvement. My speech slowly came back, my memory was intact, and the doctors viewed me as a miracle child. They told my parents that I had one chance in a million not only to survive that illness but regain my full memory and speech and not to show any side effects. Unfortunately, they had to shave my long beautiful hair, because it could not be brushed and saved after weeks of vomiting and not moving my head.

When I finally came home from the hospital, I was met with superstitious fears from my neighbors, and my former friends did not want to play with me. From what I remember, the parents of my friends prohibited them from playing with me. For all the time I was in the hospital, they knew that I was not going to make it. All of a sudden, I appeared alive, and they thought I came back from the dead. I remember going outside to play, standing alone in the yard, and children were yanked by their parents away from me. The rejection by my peers left a heavy mark on my heart. At five years old, I could not understand why my friends were mean and abandoned me and why their parents told them not to be my friend. No one cared about me, and no one explained why my friends so cruelly rejected me.

That rejection of a five-year-old left a heavy mark on my heart and for years altered my attitude toward others. Until one moment in my life, I did not know why I was so unforgiving, pushing people away if I sensed that they could hurt me. Years later, I discovered when I made this decision: when I was standing alone, un-welcome, un-supported, and rejected by all. Then I decided that I would not allow anybody to hurt me or treat me this way. I started pushing people away and ending relationships as soon as I smelled a betrayal.

So, how is this traumatic illness and experience related to a past life, you may ask? Well, let me continue.

I loved reading books by Doreen Virtue, the Angel Therapist. She wrote many books about Angels; her books are very interactive, engaging, and compelling. In one of her books, *Earth*

Angels, she described the different groups of Angels and their presence in our lives. One type of Angels that she talked about she called Walk-Ins. According to this book, Walk-Ins are souls that step in the body after the original soul for whatever reason called it quits. When I was reading the chapter on Walk-Ins, something written there made me think that it could have happened to me. When I was gravely ill as a child, and despite having little chance to survive, I did; and recovered beyond anyone's expectations. So why, what does my survival have to do with Walk-Ins? The explanation came to me many years later and in a rather unexpected way.

Although I sensed that I was a Walk-In, I did not validate my theory until I visited Tibet in 2015. I did not know why, but I always wanted to go there. It was one of the places on my bucket list. When I heard about the opportunity to travel there, I immediately agreed. Before my travels to China and Tibet, my friend asked me why I wanted to go there, but I did not have a clear answer, just replying that Tibet was one of the places I wanted to see.

During my travels in Tibet, I did not have earth-shattering experiences; I did not have any specific memories, recognition, or awareness. Even when I stepped into the monasteries, I did not feel anything beyond curiosity. I was curious how these enormous buildings, monasteries, and palaces like the Potala or Winter Palace in Lhasa, for example, were built. I was amazed to see the monumental statues of Buddhas in each monastery and learn that they were carried on donkeys and installed there. My curiosity and admiration for human abilities and the mind were at their peak throughout my journey in Tibet.

In one of the monasteries we visited, I walked into a hall with a large statue of Buddha, decorated in gold, precious stones, and gems. But what struck me were the painted walls. Each wall of this large hall was evenly divided into small squares, and each square had a sitting Buddha painted inside the square. The paintings started about a meter from the floor, and these Buddhas in the squares were everywhere. They were all the same, same colors, same pose, same face. As I mentioned, the hall was huge, the ceiling was high, and these squares were going up to the ceiling on all three walls of the monastery. As I walked around, I suddenly felt a connection to these painted Buddhas, looking at me from every corner and side of the walls. It was eerie to be watched by the painted Buddhas, but it was how I felt.

The warning signs with requests not to take photographs were posted everywhere; however, I decided to sneak a picture of the Buddha in the square on my phone on the way out. I was a little nervous not to honor the request, yet the desire to have this unusual picture back with me was more persistent. Once I snatched the picture of Buddha in a black painted square, dazzled with gold and wearing a red tunic, I felt excitement and goose (or God) bumps all over my body.

The rest of my trip to Tibet and China was fascinating and, at times, captivating. Nonetheless, nothing was as meaningful and left a long-lasting memory than that painted Buddha. His picture is with me now, it is on my phone as wallpaper, and every time I open my phone, I look at him and greet him.

But, back to the story. Shortly after coming home, I started having unexplained skin rashes that appeared to be an allergic reaction to something. This skin rash did not itch, and I only had a burning sensation, from the top of my head to my toes. Doctors had no idea what was going on, yet I continued having them more and more frequently.

Fortunately, when these symptoms began, I was a student at the University of Santa Monica once again, auditing a Consciousness, Health, and Healing program. It was timely for me to be in this healing program because the western doctors could neither diagnose nor help me treat my skin rash. However, I was determined to heal these skin rashes that stubbornly did not go away. During one of the USM weekends, we were taught a process called Healing Poetry. It was a fascinating exercise that required writing a poem about a physical, emotional, or mental issue that needed healing. Since I was still dealing with the skin condition, I thought writing a poem about these mysterious rushes would be appropriate.

And the poem was born. My first ever poetic attempt was traumatic, dramatic, and emotionally painful. It triggered a memory of being burned alive. (Again!) It was a voice of the past coming through in words and screams, pleading for help.

I had no idea where the images and words came from, though, after completing the poem, I finally pieced together my childhood illness, Tibet, and skin rashes. I realized it was one of my past existences coming through for healing. I recognized that life as a Buddhist monk, who perished as many, fighting for Tibet independence from the Chinese when they took over their country. I learned that many monks were burned alive, tragically dying for their freedom. I believed that a monk became a walk-in and entered my body when I was burning with a high fever from meningitis and was between life and death. My soul did not want to stay in the body and was ready to quit and move on.

Whether the contract was made on the soul level between the two souls (mine and the monk's), but when I put together all the events, I understood why I lost speech and was mute for two weeks (possibly because the walk-in soul had to learn a new language), why doctors shaved my hair, and I was bald like a little monk, why after I recovered from my illness I became a very serious, even a reserved child who rarely smiled or played like my peers. The cheerfulness and ease I had as a child were gone.

I also realized why Tibet was one of the places on earth I so wanted to visit. I also realized that the skin rashes that began a few days after I returned from China, totally related to cell memory. No medical doctor could explain the random rash that covered my body in bright red from head to toes and felt like being burned all over my body. The rashes only went away when I approached it from healing memories of that life and prescribing myself the right supplements that helped reduce the histamine levels during the attacks.

The skin rash eventually stopped, and for the last several years, I was free from feeling the burning sensation.

Here is the poem that became a healing agent for me.

THE MONK.

What is this? What is happening to me?
My mind is like in smoke, sending SOS messages to my body
What is happening? I am at a loss
I know that my body is on fire like I have a bad sunburn
But I am not near the beach; it is my mind that makes my body burn,
More questions than answers,
Why? What makes it burn?
My voice is quiet, but the image of life is here.

In that existence, a sleepless existence,
The fire was set intentionally and burned me
And others that were with me
To ashes.
No one heard our screams,
No one cared for us,
There was no one to care...
We were heretics; we had to be destroyed
Along with our dangerous ideas and risky words.

No one shed a tear, no kind word was spoken,
Our pains, screams, and anguish
Our curses and swears were unanswered,
Our destruction brought more darkness and harshness to the world.

CHAPTER 5

"Life can only be understood backwards; but it must be lived forwards."
— **Soren Kierkegaard**

Love-Hate or Hate-Love?

When I barely understood or knew about the concept of reincarnations and past lives, I almost accidentally discovered this particular lifetime I had with the friend of my youth. It all unfolded in the early nineties, just a few years after I arrived in the US. That friend and his family lived in the US for over ten years, and when we came to the US, they helped us integrate and assimilate into our new life. After a few years, they invited us to vacation with them and our young children in Yosemite. Although we had a strained relationship at that time, we decided to spend this vacation together.

Overall, we had a good time together, and the children had fun and adventures. I loved every moment of being so close to nature, breathing the incredibly fresh air of the pine trees, and being in awe of the mountains' beauty and majesty. Onc day they all went hiking, but I decided to stay in the cabin and rest. I turned on the TV and started watching some local talk show with the guest Brian Weiss, promoting his new book *Through Time into Healing*.

I was fascinated by the guest and the discussion they had of past lives and reincarnations. I intently listened, absorbing everything the guest shared from his research and experiences working with many patients. The whole concept of past lives was foreign to me, but my interest in the subject matter quickly made up for the lack of knowledge. I remember how the light bulb was lighting up in my head when Dr. Weiss described to people in the studio how to recognize if we had past lives together with somebody.

I was amazed and amused by everything I was learning from that program. I immediately recognized that the friend from my youth we were vacationing with was that person, and we had a past life together. I had no idea what life it was or what happened, but, like in a puzzle, the pieces came together in one moment. Our tumultuous relationship did not start when we first met when we were just 18 years old! We must have been through this before; it was apparent to me. This information, like a key, opened a hidden door for me, and I wanted to find out what happened, who I was, who he was, and how it all related to our today. My thirst for learning about past lives became unstoppable.

A few hours later, they all came back from the hike, excited and tired; I did not say a word to any of them about what I just saw on TV or shared my thoughts and suspicions. We made it through a few more days without major blowups, which was a big deal. Yet, our relationships continued to go from good to bad to worse to no relationship at all. It was exhausting and troubling at times. I wanted to understand why I could not get out of this unhealthy relationship that was toxic for my family and me, and I continued the search to understand this all and get rid of it. Later on, I bought the book by Brian Weiss and started reading, analyzing, and learning about this fascinating subject and how to help myself to get out of this maze.

My first job in the US was as a preschool teacher, and I met many wonderful parents/mothers while working there. One such parent, by the name Zina, was a mother whose child was in the class I was teaching. We became friendly, and she shared with me that she was an artist, intuitive and was doing psychic readings. I expressed interest and desire to learn about her art, and she offered to do such a psychic reading for me. I told her how intrigued I was, and my curiosity was growing every day.

Finally, I came to her home to have a reading. She explained how it works and invited me to the table, where she spread a large piece of paper and boxes of pencils. Considering how long ago it occurred (sometime in 1994), I remembered how she did the reading. I remembered her asking me questions, and, at the same time, she drew a picture of me in the middle of the paper. From that image in the middle of the list, she began drawing lines around and started speaking. Unfortunately, that artwork was lost over the years, and I do not remember much of what she said, but one thing stuck with me that I could not forget. She asked me if I had enemies because she saw the dark energy of betrayal and deceit around me. I instantly knew who she was referring to because it could only be that friend and his wife because of the regular dose of poison I experienced from them. They manage to stain and taint many things in my life, causing my family many unpleasant and even hurtful situations.

Without ever mentioning to her anything about him and his wife and our tug-of-war relationship, she right away picked on the negativity emanating from them. She then proceeded to tell me that our relationship went centuries back. She described what she saw. She said that he and I were together in several lifetimes, playing different roles and different sexes. However, the one life together as brothers was a culprit of our current life's hatred and attraction, love-hate relationship.

She described that we were farmers in that lifetime, that it was the Middle Ages in Europe. Everything she said about him immediately made sense because we had so many things in common, including our love for plants, gardening, planting, nurturing, and growing various plants.

She also described a love triangle between the two of us and a young girl that was our neighbor and mentioned that this young girl we both loved was my husband (?) in this life. And this statement made total sense to me because he and my husband were close friends, and I always felt that I competed with him over my husband. He was the best man at our wedding, and at some point, they worked together and developed a close friendship. I was annoyed by their solidarity and closeness and often felt let down by their bond. Zina told me that our relationship, like thick ropes, is entangling me; that is why it was hard to cut through and break away.

She continued telling me the story of that lifetime. She said that a young girl (my husband) preferred me and we got married. She said that he (the friend) was devastated; he enlisted in the war and was killed, never forgiving me for stealing his love and his life. She also said that we were together in other lifetimes, as cousins, as friends, but our relationships were always based on love-hate and competition. Again, what she was saying explained how in our early friendship (since we were 18), I always related to him as a sibling, as my soul brother, not even understanding my words' accuracy. Many people faded away from my life over the years, but he and I continued our dance of resentment and closeness, hatred and friendship, unforgiving and love, and then hate again.

That scenario of love-hate, getting close and pulling apart, was true for many years. Still, no matter how many attempts I have made to destroy that invisible but energetically thick rope, he and his wife managed to make a comeback into our lives. The last time I had a reprieve was about ten years, but after that long time, I had to agree to let them back into my life due to unforeseen events. That phase of the amicable relationship and friendship lasted several years. Still, old habits die hard, and our irreconcilable differences came up again, and we had another unpleasant and bitter falling out. From that moment, the connection was terminated, and I trust that it was the last time I axed that rope of toxic love-hate relationships.

CHAPTER 6

"As we go within the self, we discover that all the voices of our past lives are still there. As we peel ourselves, which is a process very much like peeling an onion, we discover that there are many selves within the self."
— **Frederick Lenz**

The Childbirth Death

The fascination of past lives in general and my past lives, in particular, compelled me to continue seeking information, reading, and exploring more on the subject matter. My interest was only growing, and with each memory showing up randomly, I wanted to bring forward more of what happened in that particular lifetime.

Books written by Brian Weiss attracted me, and I read many of them. When the Hay House Publishing Company offered a cruise to Alaska with Dr. Weiss teaching seminars about past lives, I knew I would be on this ship. And I was. It was indeed one of the most memorable experiences traveling to Alaska on a cruise ship, exploring the magnificent land, meeting people, creating friendships, and just having good times.

But the most meaningful for me was the seminars with Dr. Weiss, his teachings of past lives, and past life regressions he conducted for all partaking in his workshops. During one of the regressions, one significant lifetime came up for healing.

Every morning session Dr. Weiss began with group hypnosis, and one morning, following his easy induction techniques, I entered a lifetime in France in the Middle Ages. I saw myself as a 16-year-old pregnant wife of a wealthy man of nobility. Somehow, I knew it was my second birth, and the midwife was called to deliver the child. To my misfortune, this midwife did not have much experience, and when the baby was born, she could not stop the bleeding, and I died from the extensive blood loss, leaving my baby girl alone. It was the only piece I received during the regression; it was vivid, dramatic, and palpable.

Dr. Weiss's questions during and after regression led me to understand who is who or who was who in that lifetime. The midwife that let me bleed to death was my mother in this lifetime. It was so clear to me and immediately explained that the underlying resentment I felt from an early age toward my mother stemmed from deep-seated anger. I felt that anger toward her when I was dying, helplessly looking at my baby, knowing that she would be an orphan. I also recognized that my daughter was that baby girl that was born to grow as an orphan. The sadness and pain of that unnecessary early demise became the heavy unconscious memories I carried to this life.

That regression left me feeling like I had a punch in the gut. It was traumatic and distressing because it involved two of the most significant people in my life: the one who birthed me and the one I birthed.

I was determined to know more about that short life and its sorrowful ending. I wanted to let go of resentment toward my mother and accept what happened then, forgiving her. Maybe that's why in this life, when I, as a child, became dreadfully ill after contracting chickenpox, she could not let me die again, though I was very close to dying.

I wanted to release my need for overprotection and control toward my daughter this time because of the unfulfilled feelings of love and caring I could not give her then. I knew the painful memories of that tragic life came forward for healing and mending on all levels, and I knew I needed to get to know her so that she could tell me more about herself. When I tuned in to her after childbirth, the following picture came to my attention. It was like watching a movie on my mind's screen.

On a cold autumn day of 1674, in the house of French nobility, his young 16-year-old wife was giving birth to their second child. The first child was stillborn, and the young couple lived through grief and anguish. She was heartbroken, and he was disappointed. This time they both were anxiously anticipating the birth of their second child, praying and hoping for a better outcome. When she felt the initial labor pains, the midwife was called to help her with delivery. The midwife was familiar to the young woman because she delivered her first child, the stillborn, a year ago. However, the young woman felt uncomfortable and did not like the midwife's energy because seeing her reminded her of the failed childbirth and the feelings of loss about her firstborn.

Unfortunately, her husband was not in the house when her labor started. Fortunately, the young woman had servants around the midwife, helping her with everything she needed. The labor pains were not intense, and it did not last long, so they all anticipated that it would be over soon. The young woman already knew what to expect from the delivery process and how to act. Hence, in a short couple of hours, she already held a baby girl in her arms.

The young mother intensely held her child, looking at her with such tenderness, love, and admiration, thanking God for giving her this little miracle. At the same time, the midwife was working on finishing up the labor, suddenly realizing that she could not stop the internal bleeding after birth. The young mother, the young woman, the young wife who just birthed the best gift of motherhood, slowly was dying from the blood loss, and no one could save her. She still did not know what was happening, as she felt euphoric holding her baby and not paying attention to the sudden commotion and tension that appeared in the room. She heard that the midwife was yelling to servants to call the doctor, but the midwife's voice became more distant and softer. She did not know why she suddenly felt the overwhelming sense of peace and even joy in her heart and body. She was dying filled with love for her newborn and love for her husband. In seconds, her short life flashed before her eyes; she saw her parents, her younger brothers, and sister, whom she dearly loved and missed because they lived far away with her parents and could not see each other after she was married to her husband. She saw her stillborn first child, but now he was right there, before her eyes, and she could not understand why she saw him alive and smiling at her. What happened.? Where was she, and where was her newborn baby girl?

She floated back to see what happened, and when she saw her body lifelessly lying on the bed, she screamed, but no one could hear her screaming. The servants took over the baby, and everyone was crying. They all cried from the immense sadness of losing their kind and beautiful countess, so full of life and desire to live. They feared the wrath of their master and felt guilty and helpless that they could not protect and save her.

She floated a little longer until her beloved husband returned to their grief-stricken home and found everyone devastated and in tears. She heard the main servant telling the husband what happened to her, and she saw him almost fainting from pain and sadness. He then collected himself and asked to bring him his child. She wanted to see how he would be with the child, which caused him to lose his love. He tenderly held the baby, looking in her eyes, rocking her, and singing a lullaby. He named her Elizabeth in honor of his departed wife, Beth. Beth made a few more circles above her husband and baby Elizabeth; she knew he would be a great father to their child, and she left this earth plane, letting go of her connections to that life. She knew her daughter would be loved, cared for, and adored. She floated back to meet her son, and together, they moved toward Light.

CHAPTER 7

*"The immediate source of a mind… must be a mind which existed
before the conception took place; the mind must have a continuity from
a previous mind. This we hold to prove the existence of a past life."*
— **Dalai Lama**

The Mayan Girl

In early 2000 I read a book by one of my favorite authors, Sylvia Browne. The book was titled *Past lives Future Healings*. It was a fascinating book that I read with much interest and curiosity. Every chapter was a case study, as she called them, in which she described her work with clients on the issues that afflicted them, whether physical, emotional, or mental. Her stories impacted me greatly, and with each new one, I could see apparent connections between past lives and present incarnations.

The last chapter of Sylvia Browne's book was written as a step-by-step guide for the reader to do it yourself past life regression. When I finished reading the book, I wanted to do a past life regression following Sylvia's script but was always busy. After a while, I put it on the shelf, thinking that someday I will do a past life self-regression. I guess it was not the right time YET.

A few years passed since I read this book, and in the back of my mind, I always remembered that regression I never tried. One morning I woke up with excruciating back pain, not able to move. Going to work was out of the question, and staying in bed was my only option, and reading was one thing for me to do. Sylvia Browne's book was nearby, so I reached for it and looked through the pages, choosing some chapters to read. Then I remembered the last charter on self-regression, and it occurred to me: why not use the step-by-step instructions to find out where and when my back problem began?

I opened the last chapter and several times read the instructions to memorize the questions I had to follow. I was anxious to explore "Who I was, What happened to me, When and Where it occurred, and How what happened then affected Now" in hopes of healing the longstanding back pain. I always wanted 'to know' things; even as a child, I was curious to search for answers.

Following instructions, I closed my eyes and, using self-hypnosis, quickly entered the altered state of consciousness. I asked myself to show when and where the back problems began. At the script's suggestion, I looked at my feet and saw that I was not wearing any shoes; I was barefoot. Suddenly the whole picture unfolded in my mind; I knew I was a Mayan girl living in a Mayan village. I knew that I walked to and from the local forest every day, collecting wood and branches in the woods and bringing it back for the villagers. I saw myself carrying those piles of wood on my back, bending from its weight. My back was aching day and night, and even when I was resting, the pain was always there. I saw the animals that lived in the forest, they were my companions and friends, and I preferred them to the villagers, both children, and adults, as they were mostly unfriendly, even mean at times; they teased and shunned me. I was an orphan and was sad all the time. I felt my life was a meaningless existence, and I always felt tired.

The last question in the script was about death and the circumstances surrounding one dying. When I asked that last question, I saw an infected foot, and I knew the answer in an instance. It was death from stepping on something poisonous while walking through the forest barefoot. Seeing the image of the infected foot helped me to connect the dots between then and now. It was solid proof that everything I just saw in my mind was not a figment of my imagination.

Moreover, it was a complete validation of everything I envisioned, and I connected the dots between the life of a Mayan girl and mine based on this information. She died from walking barefoot. Up until that moment, I had no idea why I was always cautious and even afraid to walk barefoot since childhood, or as long as I remember myself. It was absolute proof, and I no longer had any doubts about the information I received.

Even as I was writing these words about the infected foot, I cringed, feeling discomfort in my body. Fascinating how cell memory works! The feeling of sadness came over me, the sorrow of a bleak life, lonely and forsaken, not missed by many, and the death that was unnoticed by all. I lived quietly, and I died with no one around. Only my animal friends missed me.

When all these memories about that life came to the surface, I started crying. I cried over that girl who no one loved, no one cared for, no one missed, and who was left to die alone. When the tears stopped, I felt some relief, but the judgments about her death, the uncaring villagers, the physical pain carried through centuries -all came up and overwhelmed me at that moment. It was such an unremarkable, sad, and short life that I felt sorry for her and myself. Why myself? Because through cell memory, I 'inherited' her physical condition in the way of back pain. This memory carried over to this lifetime, manifested in my body, became chronic, and surprisingly came forward for me to deal with and heal this time around.

Frankly, at that moment, I had no idea what to do with all these disturbing and painful memories I was drowning in. The upset was overwhelming, I felt deep compassion for this girl, for her physical pain and suffering, and this sadness did not leave me for quite some time. Then I remembered *Self Forgiveness*! Of course, it dawned on me; how could I forget the most valuable tool I've ever learned when I was a student at the University of Santa Monica. Certainly, *Self-Forgiveness* is the most versatile and helpful tool that everyone who graduated from USM uses. I immediately started saying inwardly: "I forgive myself for judging myself as unloved, I forgive myself for judging myself as undeserving of care, I forgive myself for judging myself as alone, I forgive myself for judging myself as voiceless, I forgive myself for judging myself as unwanted. The harsh words of self-condemnation came into my mind, and it felt like open cuts and stabs on my psyche. It was one of the most painful *Self Forgiveness* processes I had to do in all my years of practicing the skill.

I felt emotionally connected to this Mayan Girl; I felt her sadness, discontent, and distress. My physical and lower back pain subsided in a few days, and I returned to work, but the images of that lifetime, filled with infected foot and physical back pain, have accompanied me throughout the years.

Curiously, another validation of life as the Mayan Girl came to me on vacation in Cancun years ago. We went on the excursion to Chichen Itza Pyramids and Mayan village, exploring these historical sites. When we walked through the village with our tour guide, he told us about Mayan culture, Mayan civilization in ancient times, and people who lived in these villages and what they were doing. He specifically described how some younger villagers went into the forests to collect wood and branches and bring them back, carrying piles of wood on their backs. They were doing this to help with boiling water, food preparation, and keeping warm. Hearing the stories told by the tour guide brought images of that desolate unfortunate girl who perished quietly the way she lived.

The significance of that insignificant past life and its influence this time around is hard to underestimate. She showed me that my back injury and chronic back pain did not start 30 +years ago and that the healing of memories must begin with this Girl. And it is a life-long process of forgiving myself for all the judgments I still subconsciously carried inside about injustices and misfortune that this girl had to endure.

As I wrote the last sentence of this chapter, I thought of gestalt with the Mayan Girl. I decided to give a voice to a voiceless, unnoticed Mayan Girl, and I inwardly asked her if she wanted to speak. To my surprise, she agreed, and I asked her to speak up and tell me about her life, sadness, and pain. This is what she told me: "I was not a sad girl; I loved going to the forest and gathering branches, leaves, and flowers. Every day I saw my friends: the birds were flying around me, accompanying me on my path, singing their happy songs; the iguanas were right there, greeting me early in the mornings, and the rabbits were happily hopping next to me. Sometimes baby deer were coming on the path to greet me, and monkeys were following me around. I loved leaving the village and going to the forest, though it was cold, yet seeing a sunrise every morning brought so much joy to me. So, I was a happy girl. I did not feel lonely; I was thankful for the freedom I had."

"But what about hurting your back when carrying the wood on your back every day? I asked her.

"It's true," she replied to me; "I often felt terrible pain and sometimes even cried when I could not move in the morning. When my mother was still alive, she made me a special drink when it happened, and after drinking it and falling back to sleep, I would wake up shortly after without pain. Even though my work seriously hurt my body and back, I still loved going to the forest every day. I never got tired from seeing the morning sun, from seeing the beauty of flowers opening up with the sunrise, walking on the cold dew, and seeing my animal companions greeting me. I felt the power and magic of this magnificent place that I was a part of."

I wanted to know more and asked about people in the village and whether they cared about her. She said: "It's true, they did not care about me, I was not pretty, my mother was poor, and they did not care about either of us. I had been left an orphan when my mother suddenly died not long before me.

I helped my mother cook meals for us, and sometimes she was cooking herbal remedies to offer to the villagers. That's why carrying wood was essential for me to do. I did not mind, I wished we were rich, but I still would go to the forest but not carry wood every day, just to gather plants and flowers."

"You know", I told her, "The back pain you felt then, I feel today, though I do not carry wood from the forest, and now I need your help to heal it so that I can walk, sit and sleep without pain. I do not have that special drink your mother made for you, so I need your help".

"Continue with forgiveness," she said. "You made many assumptions about me and my life, and your judgments about my conditions you must let go because it is not your "wood" to carry. Your "wood" are your judgments that not only holding you back but holding your back. They are your lack of flexibility, stubbornness, unforgiveness, and emotional pain. That translates into physical pain, and as long as you are unwilling to release it from your back, your back will suffer. Your healing will happen when you no longer need to be right, and the judgments are gone."

I was deeply touched by her revelations about her life and surprised by how our lives connected. She taught me a valuable lesson about assumptions and how they can be to my detriment. What she said about the " wood" I carried was profound and convincing to me. I was grateful for her wisdom and for everything she shared with me. I was thankful that I listened to my intuition, thus reaching a new understanding and awareness.

CHAPTER 8

*"I've always been interested in past lives, because
they're earmarks of what creates us."*
— **Sylvia Browne**

The Cowboy and his Horse

One day in the late 90s, while shopping at Costco, I came across a book in a lovely pink cover by Doreen Virtue, *Angel Therapy*. The book called on me to pick it from the book stand and take it home. I still have this book and like to open it from time to time and read a paragraph or two to surround myself with the wisdom of Angelic energy. Since that first book, I had read many of her books, and her writings helped me foster my spiritual development (awakening) to seek and find many answers to my questions.

My USM friend Jami found out that Doreen Virtue offered a week-long Angel Therapy seminar in Laguna Beach, CA. The year was 2003, and we both were in a USM (University of Santa Monica of Spiritual Psychology) graduating class. Fortunately for both of us, the circumstances aligned so that we could both attend that seminar. Jami and I admired Doreen's writings and teachings at that time, read her books, and loved to play with her Angel Cards. We registered for the seminar and were eager to spend the whole week with Angels and learn Angel Therapy.

The atmosphere at the seminar was vibrating with high energy and created delight; excitement and joy were in the air; we were encouraged to be open to miracles and mystery. We bolstered our spiritual growth and positively increased our frequency. As I mentioned, Jami and I were a few months away from our USM graduation, and going to this Angel Therapy seminar was not only an absolute treat, but it turned out to be a powerful, profound, and transformational event for both of us.

During that week in Laguna Beach in a nice hotel on the Pacific Ocean's shore, I had many unforgettable and enlightening moments that I openly shared after daily sessions with Jami. Participating in the carefully crafted exercises and processes that I learned and practiced daily was exciting, and this work greatly expanded my awareness and consciousness. I felt the Angelic Presence and Guidance surrounding me during that week, day and night, and this high-frequency energy helped me clear and let go of many personal and generational patterns and beliefs. However, the most memorable and significant moment occurred during the past life regression group session that Doreen facilitated one day for us.

She began the session by asking us to close our eyes and guided the group through the hypnosis. When the energy in a room shifted and became soft and quiet, Doreen Virtue asked to look down at the feet to see what kind of shoes we were wearing. I learned that looking at the feet is the first step in past life regression because that helps pinpoint the lifetime that the subconscious brings forward. It's a process of sorting out Where, When, and Who.

So, when I looked at my feet, I saw cowboy boots.

How interesting, I thought, it looks like I was a cowboy that lifetime! Naturally, I was eager to learn more and carefully listened to Doreen's next direction. She told us to look for other clues, such as to see what or who is around us and if we could see where we were. As soon as she said it, I saw myself in the middle of the desert, with exotically looking cactuses around me. Wow! The vision of the desert with exotic plants triggered childhood memory and, like a missing piece of a puzzle, completed the picture. The awareness of my fascination with these strangely-looking plants finally found its explanation.

Until that moment, I did not understand why, as a young child, I was so captivated by a mysterious plant from a faraway land. I learned that this plant with needles instead of leaves is growing in a hot place. Although I kept a small cactus on my windowsill in a cold and wintery Kyiv, I dreamt of living in a place that was so warm that these cactuses would be growing on the streets. This awareness, like a lightbulb, came in a split second and brought recognition and clarity.

But back to the regression. Doreen said: Look around you and see if there is anybody you recognize from this lifetime. By looking in their eyes, she continued, you may remember them, who they are now. There was only a horse next to me, and when I looked in the horse's eyes, I immediately saw my dog, Pepper. I was astounded. I could not believe it, yet I believed it because I knew it was true. What else was true is we all jokingly called Pepper a horse.

The reason Pepper ended up in our family was his eyes. And this is how it all unfolded. In January of 1995, I came to the local pet store that held a pet adoption event that Sunday with rescued dogs and cats. I was not looking for a dog; I already had one dog and one cat. I came to buy something at the store, but I looked at the cages and dogs that were lying on the ground, waiting for their new homes. When I saw a puppy with huge eyes looking at me, I could not walk away. I learned that he was three months old, a mutt, and was found by some volunteers under the truck during the rainy week. So, there was nothing special or unique about him, yet, I decided to adopt him because of his eyes and how he looked at me. I withstood the resistance from my husband to bring home another dog, and after paying the adoption fee and filling out the paperwork, the puppy came home with us. We named him Pepper. Deep in my heart, I knew that dog belonged with me. Little did I know, we had met before.

It was a mind-blowing moment when I realized that subconsciously, all along, I knew Pepper before and knew he was a horse. My Horse. His hind legs looked like a horse; his tail was not like a dog tail, and when we talked to him, we always used to say to him, Pepper, you look like a horse. We called him a horse because of the way he would wag his tail or walk. Pepper was the gentlest and the noblest dog I ever had. He was large and awkward-looking, but his personality was sweet. When Pepper was around nine months, we started noticing that he could not walk, that he could not stand on all four, that he was trying to hold his left hind leg up. After a visit to the veterinarian, we learned that Pepper had congenital hip dysplasia. The veterinarian also told us that we had two choices: either Pepper has surgery and a plastic hip implanted for the rest of his life, or we had to put him down. He said that the dog could not live with this pain, and there was no other treatment besides surgery. The choice was apparent for us, and this is how Pepper got a plastic hip. He limped his whole life, yet he lived for almost 15 years, and though it was hard for him to get up to walk when he got older, he continued plugging along with our younger dogs and always loved to go for a walk.

After I discovered my connection to Pepper, I got even more attached and attentive to him. He was the only dog out of all my dogs that was always grateful for food. Every time I would put food bowls for them (I had three dogs most of the time), before he would start eating, he would look into my eyes as if he was thanking me for the meal. He had dark brown eyes with a gaze of a wise being that suffered a lot, and he was grateful for his whole life. Pepper died in my arms in June of 2010 from old age.

Alla Kaluzhny

After Pepper was gone, I decided to find out more details about that life and Pepper. I used self-hypnosis to regress myself to that life, and I connected with the Horse. He was a beautiful light brown horse, and his name was Cactus. He was my everything. There were two of us most of the time, we lived in the Arizona desert, surrounded by cactuses, and his name suited him ideally. One day we were caught in the shoot-out between two opposing groups, and Cactus was accidentally shot in his left hip. He fell on the side, and I slid off his back, noticing that the injury was so bad that he was bleeding to death. I could not do anything to help him. He looked at me with his eyes, filled with suffering and pain, and I knew what he was asking me to do. I fell on the ground to hug him for the last time and to thank him for all the years he was my best buddy and the most loyal friend I had all these years.

I felt his heart beating, and I heard his plea to stop the suffering. Before that time, my hand never shook when holding a gun, but I could not stop it this time. I did not have a choice but to end his pain. Through tears leaking all over my face, I had to collect my courage and all my devotion to him and take this final shot. And so, I did. I ended his suffering, and I began mine. I stayed near his body, holding him, crying, hugging, and letting all my anguish out in a final scream.

I buried my best friend in a large grave I made for him, and I left my heart in that grave with him. A few of my cowboy buddies came to grieve with me over the loss of Cactus and brought me a new young horse to train and tame. My life did not allow me to stay and mourn my loss, so I left my Cactus among desert cactuses and left his grave, forever carrying him in my heart and soul.

After I wrote about Cactus and what happened to him, everything became clear like a bell: his wound from a gunshot in the left hip and how he died, I connected to what happened to Pepper. Of course, Pepper's hip dysplasia in this life resulted from that gunshot he died from as a horse. And of course, I had to fulfill my lesson lingering from that life as a Cowboy to adopt Pepper, choose for him to have that life-saving surgery, love, and care for him his whole life, and when the time came to say goodbye to him-hold him in my arms again when he died; this time as a dog.

CHAPTER 9

*"O little one, My little one, Come with me, Your life is done. Forget
the future, Forget the past. Life is over: Breathe your last."*
— **Clive Barker**

The Ellis Island

While visiting New York about ten years ago, someone suggested visiting Ellis Island. They said that going there will be an unforgettable experience and encouraged us to take a day out of our busy itinerary and visit. I remember that the ferry line was at least one hour long; the number of people was staggering. The day we selected for this adventure was a cool late August day; it was sunny but windy. The ride on the ferry was pleasant and, in some way, special. It was fascinating to see the Statue of Liberty in front of the fast-moving ferry and skyscrapers and bridges of New York, rapidly moving away from us. On the first stop by the Statue of Liberty, we stepped out to see and experience the magnificent and ageless beauty and a symbol of new beginnings, renewed hopes, and the undying human desire to make lives better and rise above the old, the stale and the constricted.

This towering symbol of this dream was a luring promise for generations of new immigrants, including my family. As we walked around the beautiful, tenderly cared-for grounds, I could not brush off the feeling of my insignificance and smallness in the presence of this colossal statue. I did not know if my husband or friends felt this way, but to me, it was apparent. I kept thinking of the might, boldness, imagination, and determination of people who made all this possible. Were they some mental giants, able to create such a vision, birthing and bringing it to reality for future generations? What motivated them to dream such a dream, keep the faith, and be bold and fearless in the face of many adversities they had met while creating this everlasting beauty.

We could not climb the stairs because it was closed for some construction, so it was a bit disappointing not to visit the observation balcony. We could still walk around the majestic creation, looking at this colossal statue, and I felt awe all the time being there.

Our next stop was at Ellis Island. I was very curious about the Island because of how highly the people recommended it to us. I knew of Ellis Island and its role in the world at the turn of the last century but had no idea what to expect. We walked into a huge hall that, to me, looked more like an enormous train station. Crowds of people were everywhere: families, groups, tourists with guides. We could hear different languages from all corners of the large hall. We purchased tickets and proceeded to the entrance to start the tour. After waiting in line, we finally stepped into a long corridor with yellow tiles and a tall ceiling. All of a sudden, I felt tears and realized I was crying. My body's reaction was also strange; I felt goosebumps, and at that instant, I knew that I had walked through this corridor before. I could not stop the tears and felt embarrassed. I thought that everyone was looking at me, but, of course, no one did. My husband noticed that I was crying and asked what was wrong. I quietly whispered to him: I was here before. He understood what I meant and did not ask any more questions. At that moment, I had no other recollection of who I was, when and why I was there and where I came from. The answers to these questions were revealed to me later, much later.

We spent several hours walking through many rooms of this historic, emotionally charged place where sadness and fear were still palpable. We walked around carefully crafted signs, posters, and displays filled with various items, old letters, children's toys, medical instruments, and so much more. They all belonged to and represented thousands and thousands of people from different countries, cultures, religious beliefs, and faiths. Certainly, they all were different; yet, they all shared an inner desire, an idea, a dream, and a hope that the new life in this magical land can be and will be better. And this call for a better future brought them together under the same roof of this building years ago. All newly arrived immigrants who went through Ellis Island shared similar experiences of being properly vetted, checked for physical and mental health issues, criminal backgrounds, associations with communists, criminals, and other undesirable associations. Everything I read and saw was overwhelming and very emotional; however, it did not make me forget the goosebumps that flushed over my body when I walked into that one corridor.

On the way back to NY, I spent some time away from my husband and friends. I quieted my mind in an attempt to understand what happened to me at the museum. Thinking about the corridor brought back the same feeling of warmth, recollection, and remembrance. And it happened again later, no matter how many times I traveled in my memory to this place.

Nonetheless, as soon as I would think about walking through that corridor, I would immediately feel goosebumps covering my body. It appeared that I had a small child's vision, a boy dressed in winter clothes with a large scarf over his head. He seemed no older than five years old. I saw him holding his mother's hand, walking through the corridor and all the time turning back to see someone who was behind. He was dragging a little suitcase behind him, with his belongings.

Wanting to know more about this little boy on Ellis Island and what I believed was my past incarnation and the story behind it, I decided that the best way was to "talk" to him and "give him a voice." The gestalt technique I learned at USM is to dialogue with someone or something by simply asking a question and listening for the answers.

I closed my eyes and imagined this little boy in my mind. I then mentally spoke to him, asking if he was willing to talk to me. When he agreed, I intuitively told him the following:

"I see you as a little boy dressed in a winter coat and covered with a babushka over your clothes. Tell me about yourself, what's your name? Do you know where your family came from?"

The answer in my mind came momentarily.

He said:

"I came from Ukraine, and my name was Petro. My parents spoke Ukrainian, and so did I. I looked small, but when my family arrived on Ellis Island, I was seven years old. I was walking through the long corridor with my mother, and she was holding my hand. I turned back to see my family, my Batkco (father), and two older sisters. My mother and I went ahead to get in line, but I was afraid not to lose my sisters." I asked him what else he wanted to tell me. He paused and continued: "my life on the boat was so hard because I could not go anywhere. We were on the ship for a very long time, and I cried a lot because I did not want to be there. I felt scared and anxious most of the time. My Batyco was angry at me and hit me often, wanting me to toughen up. We were hungry because we did not have much money to buy food. I overheard my mother saying that she wanted to save money for America. My sisters Nastya and Anka were nauseous all that time, and I was too. ".

Why did your family leave Ukraine? I asked him. "Because my uncle was already there in America, and he wanted us to come too. My uncle and his family lived in America for seven years, and he wrote to my father that he was happy."

What happened on the Island? I asked him. " My family was allowed to go to America after we stayed on the Island for three months. We all were anxious to leave and start a new life, but suddenly my sister Nastya became ill, and we all were not allowed to leave for New

York until she got well. We all had to wait patiently because the people on the Island were very strict and did not let sick people or families inside the country."

What did you do on the Island? I asked him. " I started going to school with my sister Anka and learning to speak English. I made friends with other children from other places and countries, and we were helping each other accept and adjust to new rules and our new life.

What happened after your stay on the Island? "We left the Island on a small boat to New York, and I was both fearful and excited to meet new people, my uncle and his family I never knew. My Batyko looked everywhere for his brother but could not find him, only his family. He later found out my uncle got in trouble and was arrested while we were still on Ellis Island, but I did not know why. His family was now left without help, and my father started helping them and caring for them too. My mom had to work too, and both mother and father worked hard all day. My aunt could not work because she took care of my very sick cousin, who was now ten years old. My mom told me that he became ill on the boat on the way to America when he was a baby when they traveled. Luckily, when they came to Ellis Island, his health improved, which allowed their family to enter America.

Sadly, his condition later came back; it affected his bones, and he could not be left alone. My uncle was providing for his family with his work, but not anymore. My aunt Lusia had to sew some simple clothes and sell them to make ends meet when my uncle no longer returned home. She told my mother how worried she was, not knowing where my uncle was, but she could not even cry because it would upset my cousin, thus worsening his condition.

Life was so hard for everybody in my family that I wanted to help too. However, my mother did not want my help; she only wanted me to go to school, to become a learned man, and save my family from poverty. My mom told me more than once: "I have so much hope for you; your sisters will marry well, and this is good enough for me. But you...... you are my joy and pride, and I know you will bring our family good fortune, good name, and good status.

I grew up with the expectation my mother lovingly placed on me, and in the back of my mind, I heard her voice all the time.

For her, it was more of wishful thinking and a deep belief that her son will become successful and bring our family a "status" she dreamt about. But for me, the wishful thinking she firmly held to has become a heavy burden.

Frankly, I did not even know what she meant by "status," but the word sounded like punishment to me. I loved my mom, but at the same time, I often wanted to escape from her and her forcefulness.

All I wanted was to be and play with my friends. Studies and school were not my forte, and going to school invoked apprehension and anxiety because I barely did my homework. One summer day, I escaped forever. I drowned while swimming with my friends and jumping in the river. I hit a rock with my head and never made it up. My soul moved away from the lifeless body still in the bottom of the river, feeling relief and liberation. No more pressure of "status" and obligations to bring pride to the family. I was 12 years old at that time. My mom suffered not only the loss of her only son, her favorite child but a massive blow to her ego, hoping to earn her status. She still has my two sisters to dominate and expect something from, but it's another story."

Petro gave me a long look with these final words, and I knew our communication had ended. I felt an overwhelming sadness for this boy and his family's hapless life, and knowing what I just learned gave me a clear picture of why I was crying while walking through that corridor at Ellis Island. Subconsciously I knew nothing good would come out of this place, that the dread and hopelessness will follow, ending tragically for all. It seemed that the boy did not even have a bright day in his short life. Everything life brought him was disheartening and burdensome. After our communication, I felt a strong connection to him and decided that healing this memory is my responsibility. He died carrying with him so many judgments to the other side that forgiving and releasing these judgments would not only heal him but uplift me and clear my energy.

I inwardly talked to him again and asked if he would be willing to clear the bad feelings he died with. Petro frowned at first but then smiled, and it was the first smile I saw. I only hinted to him what judgments are, and he immediately began telling me as if I pulled a plug from his bottled-up emotions pushed deep down. This is what he said:

"I blamed my father for his meanness and anger.

I blamed my mother for letting him mistreat my sisters and me.

I blamed my mother and father for moving us away from our homeland, thus bringing misery and misfortune to all.

I blamed my uncle for getting in trouble with the law and making my family look after his family.

I resented my ill cousin because everyone was walking on the eggshells around him as he was the most important person on earth.

I blamed myself for not being tough enough and did not cry over my sadness and nostalgia.

I blamed my mother for not protecting me and only wanted me to please her and bring "status."

I blamed myself for my weaknesses and fears.

I blamed myself for my bad grades at school and

I blamed my teacher, who did not like me and constantly humiliated me in class.

I blamed myself for not speaking good English and for not learning to speak fast enough.

I blamed myself and my mother and father for so many other things."

He paused and became teary.

Do you want to continue? I asked. I waited for his response and noticed that I was yawning and could not stop, as if I was sleepy. Then I realized that I was releasing his bottled-up negative energy, and his words felt heavy and intense to me. After a short pause, he said he felt complete, and I thanked him for his courage to be willing to speak out. Then I told him about forgiveness and explained that only forgiveness could heal what happened to him over one hundred years ago. He agreed and said: " I forgive everyone who ever wronged me and hurt me. I forgive myself for my weaknesses and feeling small. I forgive myself for never living up to my mother's expectations of me. I forgive all."

I continued to yawn. I felt goosebumps all over my body with his every word, realizing that the deep healing was happening on my subconscious and conscious levels. Yawing did not stop for a while, as I thanked Petro again, and he was gone. I felt tenderness and deep compassion toward this child whose life was cut short and his parents and sisters who left with holes in their hearts. This child did not come to a new country on his own, his parents brought him without his consent, hoping for a better life, but he did not live long enough to experience success.

I knew it was time to let go of that life's memories and bring light and gratitude for everything that just happened. I suddenly felt lighter and ready to put that life memory to rest. I felt complete, took a deep breath, and, not surprisingly, the yawning stopped.

And So It Is.

CHAPTER 10

"True healing must come first at the Soul level... prayer aligns our souls with God... By aligning ourselves with God - this highest possible state of unconditional love, joy, and wholeness - we can overcome anything, be healed of all afflictions."
— Rosemary Ellen Guiley

The Scribe

Reading, studying, or knowing about The Bible was never on my to-do list. Growing up in a communist country, where religion was basically outlawed, I was raised, like millions of children in the former Soviet Union, to despise religion, church, and God. Most churches in Kyiv, where I was born and grew up, were destroyed, with only a few open, for deeply religious older people to attend. It was even forbidden to baptize a child, and if some families were brave enough to go against the government rule, they often risked harsh punishment and jail for their disobedience and defiance. One memory comes to mind from my childhood to describe how brainwashed I was by school, education and society in general. When I was 13, I fractured my hip and was hospitalized for several weeks. In the hospital room with me were four or five girls with different traumas. One day, a girl with a broken arm was admitted to our hospital room, and at first, everyone was friendly and pleasant toward her. She was very nice too. However, shortly after she came, one of the girls overheard her father was a small church pastor outside of Kyiv. As soon as we learned this, we all immediately turned on her, treating her with scorn and animosity. We did not tell her why our attitude toward her suddenly changed, but the meaner we were, the more overly kind she was with us, which in turn, made us collectively even more suspicious toward her. It was such a contradiction: on the one hand, we liked her; she was generous and kind; on the other hand, we hated her because of who her father was, and his connection with church immediately made her "wrong" and "repulsive." As children, we were taught, and it was drilled in our heads from a very young age, that religion was "bad" and that there was no God and everything associated with the church was wrong. We could not help ourselves but act out the indoctrination we all accepted as truth. I remember that after she was discharged from the hospital, we felt such a relief because we all, collectively, perceived her lower than, with disdain. So, in retrospect, I can say how powerful propaganda worked on innocent children who grew up in a closed society that did not allow any dissent, any independent thought that differed from the official opinion.

From this glimpse into my past, my relation toward religion and the Bible was understandable. At least for me. A few years ago, the Bible's topic came to my attention during a phone conversation with Nina, one of my friends. I remember driving back from work one day and speaking with her. As usual, we discussed different topics, and then Nina talked about the Bible and her studies. She liked to reference the Bible in her conversations and then asked me if I read the Bible. The words that immediately flew out of my mouth surprised and bewildered me. I heard myself saying:

"I did not have to read it; I wrote it."

"What? What did I just say? I asked Nina. "I wrote the Bible?"

I nervously laughed because such a bold and outrageous statement about myself left me feeling perplexed. I did not know how to deal with this new information about myself and make sense of it. Linda was also surprised by my statement but said that it was possibly my past life memory suddenly appearing in my consciousness. I did not even think of such a possibility. She then talked about reincarnation and said she was aware of at least two lifetimes she and I had together, but these lifetimes had no connection to the Bible. I glossed over her sudden disclosure because I wanted to continue talking about what I just learned.

As we continued talking, I saw an image of a nicely dressed young man sitting in a well-lit room by oil lamps over a large book, diligently writing something. This image appeared in my mind when I was still driving and talking to Nina. I shared with her what I saw. Besides this image, nothing else came to my awareness, and I was not propelled or interested in uncovering more.

Over the years, my interest in learning the Bible remained low, and I only knew what a couple of my friends shared with me about a Psalm or a passage or a story they felt compelled to mention from the Bible. I never initiated these conversations, and everything they told me came from their desire to enlighten me.

I seemed satisfied with not knowing more about a young man's life until one day, on one of the sites I was looking at, I saw a picture of a man that reminded me of the image I saw years ago in my mind. The picture was titled A Scribe. Hm, I thought to myself, what does it mean? I still did not seem interested in exploring more and decided to put it aside until the right time.

More time passed, and recently I was reminded of this life when I was working on this book. Suddenly I felt unexplainable resistance to writing, and it was both uncomfortable and unproductive. I needed to figure out what was going on, and after a few empty days that turned into unfulfilled weeks, I decided to find out what was going on and have a little chat with my Inner Writer. I needed to get clarity on what was holding me back. Quieting my mind and inwardly asking a question to show me reasons for feeling resistant to writing placed me in an altered state of consciousness. The answer appeared in my mind's eyes, and I was surprised to see an image of a young man in ancient-looking garb that instantly reminded me of a Scribe, the image I saw a few years before. Then other pictures formed in my mind. I was back in the same well-lit room with a massive table and large-sized books placed on it. Some were open, and a few were closed. There were feathers on the table and other things unfamiliar to me. However, the young man, the Scribe, was not there. When I noticed that I could not breathe, I realized I sensed the room's stale air. It appeared it was a while before anybody stepped into the room and was doing anything there.

"Is this the reason I feel resistant to write? "- Yes, I heard the answer. "What happened to this man? Where is he, and why is he not writing in the book? "- "He died", came the answer. At that moment, I felt overwhelming sadness and goosebumps all over my body, and I knew the time was NOW to learn about that lifetime.

It was time to connect with the Scribe, to get to know about him and his heart desires, and heal the impacts his life might've had on me today.

Even before delving into the Scribe's life, I intuitively knew that this exploration would require more tenderness, gentleness, a deeper connection to myself, and compassion for this young man and his journey. My curiosity about this young man spiked; I was sensing that his life may hold the key not only to my resistance to writing but to other issues yet unknown to me. I wanted to make him alive in my memory, and one day, when it was quiet and peaceful in the house, I decided to invite him to speak with me and tell me all he wanted to say.

When he stepped forward in my mind's eye, he appeared tired, pale, as if someone sucked life itself out of him. I suddenly felt pain in my solar plexus, and I knew it was not mine; moreover, it was his feeling of sadness and powerlessness I was experiencing as my physical pain. All of this happened before our communication.

I thanked him first of all for agreeing to our communication, and he just nodded his head, smiling. He asked me why I think he could help me with anything. I asked his name, and he said he was Nathaniel. He told me he was born and grew up in Spain, in a large family of a very wealthy Jewish moneylender. He said he was the fourth child in a family, and he was the oldest of three brothers. He said he had three older sisters and two younger brothers. Education was the most valuable asset in his family, and his parents made every effort to educate him and his sisters and brothers. They all received religious and secular education because wealthy Jews were a big part of Spanish upper society; therefore, being educated was highly important for their future and place in society.

Nathaniel fondly remembered his childhood, his parents, sisters, and brothers. He said he was the closest to his older sister, who was older than him by two years. Her name was Raquel, and she was his favorite. Nathaniel said that his father especially adored him because he was the oldest boy, and as the oldest son, he had an important role in the family. However, Nathaniel was more attracted to religious studies, and he spent many more hours studying the Old Testament than his sisters and brothers. He dreamt about becoming a writer, a scribe so that he could learn God's word and be close to God at all times. Before his Bar-Mitzvah, he had a dream that stayed with him his whole life, he said. He paused for a moment as if deciding if I was worthy to hear his dream, and then he said: 'the night before my Bar-Mitzvah Day, a big Angel came to me. I dreamt that He woke me up and said that somebody was waiting for me. He swooped me in his enormous wings, and up and up we went. The feeling of lightness and peace took over my body, and I was ready to fly with this Angel forever. But then he brought me to a big gate, and when he touched it, it opened wide. The Angel carefully placed me down on something that felt very soft, and then I heard a voice coming from everywhere. The voice spoke to me and called me by name. The voice said: My son, I have chosen you to write My Word. I want you to write My Word as many times as possible, and I want you to write it for now and for the future. You have a special gift, a talent, and I bestow your unique power, and you will become the best in delivering and scribing My Word. Remember how much you are loved, my son, and how strong you are. Remember to call on me for your mastery and inspiration." At that moment, the voice was gone. The Angel came to me again; he pulled a feather out of his wing and handed it to me. He said it was his gift to me from him; with this feather, I will be writing the Word of God.

I woke up trembling and excited. My body felt different; it was lighter and more expansive. I remembered every word, every move that happened in my Divine dream. To my amazement, I saw a feather lying next to my pillow. At that moment, I knew it was not a dream. I was blessed with an extraordinary trust and special responsibility to carry on the Word of God, and from that time on, my studies became even more serious and diligent. I became the most learned out of all my sisters and brothers in the family, and once I was old enough to start transcribing God's books, I asked my father for permission to begin. My parents noticed my undeniable passion for studying, and they saw that social life had little interest for me. So, when I approached my father for his blessing, he reverently gave it to me.

Several years passed, and I became even more prominent in the community of scribes and writers of God's books, dedicatedly working long days during these foundational times. I always sensed my Angel's presence around me, and if the physical affliction of tiredness was taking over my body, I would summon him to revive my body because my spirit was eternally high. The feather I found on my bed after the dream was also always with me, and miraculously, this feather never wore out. Holding it in my hand felt as if God was moving it and writing with me and for me. I was blessed to write with my left hand, which made my scribing even more effective and powerful. I lived my life in service to God, and I can humbly say that I lived my life's purpose by serving God."

I was moved, touched, and even impressed with Nathaniel and everything he decided to share with me. He told his story about years as a scribe on a high note, yet, it was contradictory to how he initially appeared. I pointed out this contrast and asked him.

The answer in my mind was instant, as he explained the following. He said that the way he emerged was before his transition when he was on his deathbed. He asked if I remembered the smell of stale air in the room with books but no one around. He quietly said that his years of scribing and staying in rooms without much sunlight and fresh air weakened his lungs, and he eventually succumbed to tuberculosis. He said that his Angel was with him, helping him cross, and he was never afraid of leaving the frail body. He said that everything he learned, his unique qualities, skills, and God's written word, was with him when he passed. He scribed the Old Testament, the Holy Bible, countless times, which made him so close to God that he breathed and lived by this connection.

Nathaniel said that most of the time he worked alone, scribing the Holy texts. However, he later decided to invite other scribes as apprentices to work with him, and when his illness started to develop, he knew he needed help. Nathaniel said his baby brother Jacob, who was ten years younger, liked scribing the books and was interested in them. That is when

Nathaniel decided to teach him the craft, and for some time, Jacob was honestly trying to help his brother and worked with him. However, the baby brother did not have the same reverence, patience, and simple interest to pursue this lifetime commitment. Jacob loved writing his own poems and stories and grew to be a writer and a poet. Jacob was very popular in a place where they lived and had a very active social life, unlike Nathaniel, who loved his solitary life and cherished his closeness to God.

Nathaniel said that Jacob was incarnated and is now one of my friends. I was surprised to hear this unexpected admission and hurriedly asked if he could name him. Nathaniel did not give me any other information but said I would eventually recognize him or her. I was perplexed. Then Nathaniel proceeded to tell me about me. He said: "I know about your writing project, and this aspiration and desire to write originated from my life. You love writing; it is your life purpose, and what you write is deep and thoughtful. I also know how you are overcoming the challenge of writing in a non-native language, and I want to commend you for taking this task upon yourself. I know that recently, you lacked consistency in writing. I was pleased when you realized that your resistance to writing was more than just usual procrastination and was more subtle and not easily identifiable. Now I can tell you that the reason behind your resistance was FEAR. Memories of sickness and death triggered your subconscious fear of prolonged writing, and I was the one who brought this subconscious memory forward for you to learn it and heal it for the last time. I know it makes no sense what I am saying right now; however, hear me out. Toward the end of my life, I felt a mixture of fear, along with judgments and regrets. I knew that long hours of dedicated working, scribing, and breathing that stale air led to my premature passing. I also had many judgments about not completing my work and leaving it to others. That is why I wanted not only to release my judgments but help you to release the unconscious fears that hold you back and prevent your naturally liquid writing. I loved learning through scribing and teaching younger people to scribe; it was my passion, and I greatly influenced the future by writing and preserving God's Word. Your writings will affect the present and future as well, but more importantly, it is impacting the past. As strange as it sounds, by exploring and reviving past lives, you help each of these memories heal; you give us a voice and do it with respect, compassion, interest, and wisdom."

Nathaniel continued: "Now you know that when you blurted out to your friend that you did not have to read the Bible because you wrote it, you were completely sincere and honest in your statement. Now you know the rest of the story. You know God's word, it's in your cell memory, but it lies dormant. You know you can awaken it by reintroducing yourself to the Holy texts to make your life even fuller, more vibrant, and inspiring. But even if you don't, you are serving God in your own way, you are close to God, and you receive Divine guidance and support.

I loved the story from your childhood in the hospital room. I wanted to cheer you on how accurately you described what happened to young impressionable minds when they are spoon-fed lies and received negative instructions full of deception. The child you singled out in the hospital had no other sin than having a father that served God. Look how many years it took for you to unlearn an atheistic ideology, cultivate your trusting relationship with God, and grow stronger in your Faith. You can always call on me to boost confidence and creativity and co-create your writing projects with God's blessings. And So it is."

With these words, Nathaniel gracefully bowed to me, and our communication was complete. His presence and charisma stayed with me, and I felt how blessed I was to have known about this life. I received another piece of a precious glass in the kaleidoscope of my past lives, and with this knowledge, I felt more enriched, complete, and inspired. I was inspired to continue this incredible journey of exploration and discovery for my highest good.

CHAPTER 11

"It's as though the words are trapped, buried under past fears, past lives, like fossils compressed under layers of dirt."
— **Lauren Oliver**

The Earthquake Death

The memory of this lifetime suddenly appeared to me in 2016, when I was a student at the Consciousness, Health, and Healing program (known as CHH) in the USM community. On that particular day, the class listened to the lecture on the 8th Chakra, its deeper meaning, and the lessons this Chakra brings. As usual, after the talk, we, the students, moved into groups of three for the trio process to work on and heal the issues associated with the 8th Chakra. (About chakras and specifically about the Eight Chakra, I will speak a little later).

When it was my turn, I moved to a client's chair (each group is rotating, and every participant has a chance to be a facilitator, silent observer, and a client). I've been doing these trio processes for the last fifteen years since I started USM, and I did not anticipate anything unusual this time. However, when it was my turn as a client to answer the exercise questions, I had a strange unwillingness to say anything or cooperate. Something inside me invoked resistance to the facilitator, and I could not overcome my feelings. Whether it was distrust toward her or apprehension, the feeling was unfamiliar to me in this setting. It felt as if I hit a wall. I felt that wall was in front of me, and I could not see the exit.

I attempted to center myself to calm down, but I was getting even more agitated and uncomfortable. I felt like I wanted to run away from that chair, that I was somehow in danger if I stayed. To my embarrassment, for the first and only time at USM, I had to ask for assistance from faculty. When a faculty assistant spoke to me, I explained that it felt like I hit a wall and could not do a trio process with that student. It was an unpleasant situation:

I felt bad for the student I just rejected, but I felt worse inside myself and appeared I had no control over what was going on with me.

When the faculty assistant asked if I would like to work with her, I agreed. I tried to put into words the confusion I was in and described an image I had. I felt there was a wall in front of me, and I could not find an exit. She listened to me with compassion, understanding that I was not whining or making stuff up. I think she recognized that in a way, I did hit a wall and realized that I was dealing with something that happened to me in another life. She masterfully, step by step, helped me to untangle that ball of confusion and upset. Then in my mind, I saw a door, a tall door, that suddenly disappeared because the walls fell on it and there was no longer an exit. The pictures flooded my mind, and like a backward movie, I began seeing what was unfolding before the door disappeared under the rumble.

Not only did I see frightening scenes, but my body was physically reacting to the images in my mind. I started shaking, and it scared the heck out of me. The faculty assistant, Lilian, spoke to me in a very calm, quiet voice, wanting to reach my conscious mind because what was happening was obviously on a semi-conscious level.

When physical shaking lessened, Lilan asked me to describe to her what I saw. Still visibly upset over what just happened, I told her what I saw. I told her that I saw a young girl, maybe 16-17 years old, sleeping in bed in a large house. She was woken up by violent shaking and loud sounds coming out of the earth in the early morning hours. The girl was terrified, I told Lilian. With another violent earth shake, she found herself on the floor, thrown out of bed.

She was panicking and crying but quickly got on her feet and started running toward the door, but did not make it. Right at that moment, the loudest roar came from beneath the earth, followed by a furious shake that took all the walls down. The falling roof crushed the girl, covering her body with broken stones, leaving her body deformed. She screamed from excruciating pain, and then the screams became weaker, turning to moans. There was no one to come and help her because the whole island and its inhabitants suffered a similar fate. Their cries and screams were heard from every part of the island, but no one came to their rescue. The girl felt intolerable pain all over her crushed body and was losing consciousness from shock and bleeding. The Soul quickly moved and lifted away from her, hovering above, watching the soon-to-be lifeless body, deciding that it would be the best to give this body to cease. The Soul saw that there was no life possible with the injuries the young girl suffered. The Soul made a few circles above, and without any regret, it moved on. It felt that the Soul was young and even careless, and like a young child leaving a broken toy, she left a broken body. At that moment, the girl took her last breath.

All these images and memories appeared in my mind and resonated throughout my body, with goosebumps, tears, and shaking. After experiencing that lifetime ending in such a heart (and bone) breaking way, I understood my resistance and unwillingness to work in a trio. It seemed as if my subconscious mind desperately tried to keep me from relieving that painful memory of that life's end and the Soul's departure from the broken body. However, the information we studied in class served as a catalyst and has triggered my unusual reaction, igniting the cell memory.

Like a fight between two parts inside of me, one standing guard and trying to protect me from harm, the other knew I was ready.

I was ready to face the traumatic memory that suddenly surfaced from the bottomless well of the collective subconscious to be healed. Because it happened when I was in USM, the safest and the most supportive place to deal with something frightening, traumatic, and unexpected that could surface during our "working the process" exercises. This time it was the ancient past that threw me off my kilter and demanded undivided attention.

That attention and support I received from Lilian, the faculty assistant, who walked me through the exercise, helped me begin the healing process and integrate the recovered memory into the present. When it was time to complete the trio, the students had a few minutes to take notes of their experiences. When I started writing, the words, surprisingly, turned into rhymes.

Here is what I (?) wrote:

I slept and dreamt that I was flying,
But shaking earth broke off my dream,
The shaking was or so violent,
That I was shocked when tossed from bed.
I cried from fear, but no one heard me
The roof was falling; walls had crumbled
The trap was set, with no exit to free me
And let me outside.

I stopped to breathe when fear took over me,
The end is near, said startled heart,
The last I felt was violent shaking,
The last I heard was roaring earth,
My body hurts, my body broken,

Deformed and crippled, trapped inside,
My life is over, no more freedom
To live, to laugh, to dream, and love.

I see my Soul; she now leaves me,
My Soul is leaving me for good,
She takes my pain and wipes my anguish,
She might be happier next life.

When I wrote this poem, it felt like a culmination of everything I felt on that day. Even though it was strange to express myself in such an unusual (for me) manner, I did not give much thought to it then. I saved the notes from that class in a binder and did not remember about it for years. When I started working on this book and writing this chapter, I remembered the poem I wrote about that life and found the notes in my old school binder. Reading it now makes me think that the poem sounds a bit amateurish and clumsy.

But then, I thought, "Who really wrote this poem, and from where it came?" That thought came as a big surprise, and I decided to meditate on this question. Asking this question propelled me to look at this poem from a completely different angle. I believe that it did not come from me; it came through me. The poem came out of the cell memory, retelling what happened to her, not me. Was she a poet? When this idea crossed my mind, the body immediately responded by the familiar flash of goosebumps.

At that point, I felt the need to speak to her and get to know her.

Through the poem, I only learned about her death, but what about her life? The image of a young, beautiful girl, dressed in a toga, with a golden band around her forehead, appeared before my eyes. She was slim, dark-haired, with large, olive-shaped eyes, a small nose, and a bright smile. She seemed to be personable, vibrant, and wholehearted. She was in a group of young people and was the center of attention at that moment in time. Other young people listened to her as she spoke to them; they seemed attentive to what she was telling them. Then I heard her infectious laugh and the voices of young people calling her "Agatha, Agatha, read us your latest poem about love!" She smiled at them and passionately started reciting her poem. One of the young men with piercing eyes was looking at her with such admiration and tenderness that I waited to see how she would reciprocate, and when their eyes met, she looked at him affectionately and warmly. They appeared to be in love.

After I saw her surrounded by friends, she next appeared alone and told me how happy she was all her life until her last breath, when she perished under the ruins of her house. I called her Agatha, the name her friends called her, and asked her to tell me about herself.

"My parents loved me, my family adored me, my friends supported me, and I died loved." She sighed and paused. "When I knew it was the end and saw my Soul circling above my broken and deformed body, the immense sadness was the last I felt. My Soul did not want to stay around and have me survive and heal. The injuries were so severe that I would never be the way I was a minute before the earth rumbled. My 'Soul chose the exit that did not involve more suffering from a broken spine and squashed lungs. Now I am grateful she made this choice. No one could fix me, only death."

Listening to her, I felt the intensity of her emotions; her sadness and anguish took over me, and I, too, felt as if I was crushed. She said that her lover succumbed to his injuries and died like her. Many more shakings demolished the island she lived on, and many many inhabitants of the island, including her parents, died.

I wanted to help her heal the pains she endured before her last breath, and I believe these pains lingered over the lifetimes, catching up with me this time. I suspect that my body's current spine and lung conditions could be carried through millennia for healing for the last time.

I asked Agatha if she had any regrets or judgments over the tragedy that happened with her and her loved ones. She gave me a long look gazing through me, seeking the answer in a far-away past. She shook her head NO moment later, confirming that she did not have either regrets or judgments. She wisely said that the tragic end of her and the lives of her loved ones did not determine everything that happened before that fateful early morning. "I could not judge nature; that earthquake happened to all of us on the island; we perished because it was God's will. How could I blame or judge God for what happened?" Agatha asked. "I loved my life. It was easy, peaceful, and exciting. The island's unique conditions and spiritual atmosphere promoted people's talents and creativity; we lived beautiful lives caring, loving, and supporting each other. The only regret I might name is that Alexander, the love of my life, was not with me and died alone like me. I wished we would die together, embracing each other."

What else could I add to her story? Coming from her own words, Agatha's life was enchanting; she was vibrant, lively, and lighthearted. It seemed she was genuinely admired by many in her circle, and even though her end was so sudden, premature, and tragic, Agatha's life was a success. She was charismatic and powerful in life.

I now think the Soul's decision to leave Agatha's body, allowing her to expire, was out of deep compassion for her. She did not want her physical body's suffering and pains, thus letting things complete naturally.

Looking into Agatha's life and death, I am intrigued by why this life showed up for healing that day in USM class and its lessons. What qualities, if any, the Soul brought to this life for me to use, develop and enhance. Not coming from the desire to toot my own horn, I can cautiously suggest her talent, creativity, and charisma blended into my personality, and I feel grateful for such. However, it appears that my main lessons were to heal the physical body; that is why the memory of her being broken by the earthquake came to me in class. I would suggest that the physical pain could be the last imprint in the cell memory that the Soul is taking to the next incarnation. It became even more curious when I thought about the timing of the physical challenges I started to experience in this life.

In the previous chapter, I already described how severely I fractured my hip when I was 13 years old, coming down on the sled from a dangerous hill. The sled was fast approaching an old, large tree, and I was about to crush my head and probably die. The sled shifted to the side in a split second, and my hip met the tree with full force. It was a miracle, and I believe that it was a Divine intervention that I did not die that day. But I paid a high price for that one-time sledding adventure. My hip bone was brutally crushed, and repairing the fracture required some drastic measures. Following hospitalization, lengthy rehabilitation, and recovery, that fracture took months to heal, and even today, I am living with the destructive consequences of that incident that affected my spine and overall health. I do see the direct connection between Agatha's end of life and what happened to me, and I believe it was a continuation but on a lesser level with better chances of survival and healing.

The perplexing question inevitably raises about mystical relation between past life and the subject of Eight Chakra. At this point, I think it is necessary to gain clarity on this subject. I trust that nowadays, the concept of seven chakras is mainstream, and everyone reading this book is well aware of them and what roles they play in our lives. However, the Eight Chakra's purpose and its lessons are not widely known, and it would be appropriate to say a few words and find the explanation for myself. According to Carolyn Miss, the famous author, who's book *Anatomy of the Spirit* we studied in USM, the Eighth Chakra is the energetic Center of Divine Love, and the lesson of this Chakra is to Integrate the Self. It is a "portal of higher awareness." One of the purposes or opportunities associated with this Chakra includes cleaning the karmic residue. Many other matters are associated with this Chakra, and learning more deeply about it could trigger a healing memory, as it happened for me.

And years later, re-reading the handout from USM, I undoubtedly see why this memory came back roaring and shaking me to the core. I understand how it was triggered and what exactly in the written material and teaching presented in class provoked such a sudden reaction in my being. As I mentioned earlier, I am grateful for everything that happened that day. The support I received from the faculty helped me ground my memory and begin the healing process of that trauma. I also think this lifetime showed up that day because of the Eight Chakra's connection to the Soul. I believe it was my Soul that orchestrated the whole event to expand my consciousness, bring awareness and new understanding. And most importantly, to facilitate healing. Today I can attest that its mission was successful, and I am thankful for the lessons learned. I also want to add that knowing the poetic gift of Agatha, I am hoping to tap into her talent and begin writing poetry. I am curious to see what we could co-create together. I think that such cooperation can offer more opportunities for healing and create something amazing for the highest good of all. And So It Is.

CHAPTER 12

"You know, I think I had my first past life recall when I was 7."
— **Shirley MacLaine**

Resurrecting the shame

Even thinking about delving into writing this chapter stirred up feelings and emotions that I would rather suppress than express. I could not start, looking for excuses why I could not, and then wrote several different versions of the first paragraph, but none felt sincere. I questioned my readiness and willingness to recover and resurrect the memory of this past life and knew that it would take self-reflection, honesty, and vulnerability. I'm still unsure I have enough guts for this exploration of a life I wish I did not live or at least did not remember. However, for my own sake and for the sake of completing karma and clearing the memory, I decided that facing the dread and unpleasantness of digging into this lifetime is my only option. I may not be ready to empathize with and accept that past life, yet I felt the need to at least face the disturbance and anxiety it created in me. And no matter how painful they seem to be, seek self-forgiveness with ultimate spiritual healing.

So, what stirred up that "pot" filled to the rim with remorse, regrets, and shame? The answer lies in my childhood memory of when I was around ten years old, constantly feeling tired, needing rest, and not knowing why. I was so tired of being tired that one day I inwardly asked: "I wonder who I was in my last life, that I am so tired this time?" Before that moment, I did not remember having any inner conversations, especially phrasing a question about a past life, while never knowing anything about that concept was rather weird. Even more strange was a response I heard in my head from an unknown source, "a prostitute." What part of me knew about past lives when I was ten, born and raised in the atheist Soviet Union? What was the other part that replied to such an unusual question with an even more bizarre answer? But I think the most interesting of all was my reaction to this internal dialogue: neither the question nor the answer bewildered me at that time. I guess the ten-year-old found the answer reasonable enough and accepted it.

And now, I think that the life I did not want to remember calls on me to shift my perception from bitter to better, be a bigger person, like my ten-year-old, and accept the past—that past life that I labeled shameful. I think I am ready now to dive into unknown darkness, hopefully, shed light on WHAT happened to her, WHY it happened, WHO she was, and HOW we/I can make amends. Frankly, after writing all previous chapters, I don't remember such hesitancy and reluctance to begin. What am I afraid of now? What am I afraid to uncover?

When I was writing the previous sentence, all of a sudden, I felt a familiar wave of electricity all over my body, and I knew that she was right here with me, ready to speak. At this time, I did not have to ask any questions because she forcefully stepped forward and began talking to me.

"I know you are ashamed of me, thus projecting this shame on yourself, though what I did and how I lived my life had nothing to do with you, Alla. You are your own person, and in no way can you be responsible for how I or any one of your previous or future lives were or will be lived. The burden you are carrying is not yours, so you need to stop dramatizing something you had no control over because it did not happen to you. And to be honest, how many events in your now-life do you have control over, really, ha? Not too many. As much as you would like to pretend that you create your own reality, you know, it's not so; it's mostly a mirage. Your rumbling above about how hard it was for you to face your judgments about me and my life is silly, pathetic, and feeble. Really. What are you lamenting about, Alla? I did not live my life in shame nor disgrace. I did what I had to do, don't you? You judge me for using my body and selling it to get what I wanted, so what? Don't be holier than thou, because you had to compromise in your life many times too. I had to compromise also, and the form of compromise I chose was service, i.e., adultery. Remember, that service comes in many different ways. For me, it was a practical necessity. I felt no shame or guilt; I was in demand, worshiped, and adored.

Yes, my life was short, but it was entertaining, busy, and dazzling. Men adored me, and many wanted to be with me, seeking my affection and service. I did not care about any of them; for me, they all were a vehicle for a more opulent and influential life, which I greatly desired. They used me, and I used them, and I did not find anything wrong, moreover shameful with these arrangements. I sought power and influence, and this lifestyle gave me all I wanted. Yes, I was tired from time to time because I was so in demand that sometimes I had to forgo rest and sleep."

She stopped to catch a thought, and I felt a little shell shocked. I was just scolded and smacked by myself from the past. How do I even characterize what happened? The thoughts swarmed and buzzed inside my brain; I wanted to ask her questions, but she was not about to follow my script; she was so authoritative and strong, and she wanted to do things her way, wanting to lead, not be led.

"Do you want to know my name, Alla?" she asked, "My name was Lily. Like a flower. A white, gorgeous, elegant flower: the symbol of beauty and innocence. And innocent I was. Despite what roles I played, inside, I was innocent. Along with all other qualities I mentioned above.

They used my body but could never reach my soul, my inner flower. I was born in Russia and came from a family of performers; I grew up in a theater my father owned, and from an early age, I performed, danced, sang, played musical instruments, and was great at entertaining others. I was talented and learned to play different roles in my father's theater. My popularity and success were like a pebble in a shoe for many, including my older sisters. Like Cinderella, I was surrounded by envying sisters who could not stand me or my surprising fame."

She finally made another pause as if she was unsure if the story about her siblings and family was to be shared. I wanted to inject a comment but decided to bite my tongue and let her continue. Everything she was saying about herself and her life was utterly opposite from who I assumed she was all these years. How ironic that I felt shame over something that did not happen and preferred to focus on the worst assumptions. Oh, those negative fantasies! Occasionally, I catch myself in a world of negative future fantasies, and ironically, I was there again!

"You want me to tell you about my family and my sisters, right?'. She asked me. I nodded in response. " Almost always, I was the center of attention, even when I was a young child. I was the second talented child in a family; Andrew, the oldest child, was the most brilliant, outstanding, and prominent out of all of us. Not only was he a great actor, he wrote his own music, had a fantastic voice and sang his original songs. Andrew had that special magnetism that made everyone want to be with him or around him.

"What about your other siblings?" I asked her. She frowned momentarily and said she did not like them like they did not like her, and sibling rivalry was constant between them. She said the sisters were good performers, but their jealousy and competition were so toxic that it was spilling over, poisoning their relationship. They could not stand Andrew's brilliance, but I was the one that got the worst of their bitterness, unfortunately, and they tormented me anytime they could. Because they mistreated me and my powerlessness as a child, I craved power, craved revenge, and growing up, I promised myself never to be or feel powerless. And this desire for revenge, coupled with my inherited talents, artistry, and entertaining abilities, became a driving force for my choices and decisions.

Because of my sisters' cruel treatment, I grew a thick skin, which ultimately made me influential and forceful. I had to become audacious and bold in reaching the goals I planned for myself. I pursued importance and wanted to dominate not only over them but over others who mistreated me, or who I thought had mistreated me. So, this is how I decided that my long-planned goals for fame, glamour, and domineering could become my reality through intimate relationships with men. And they did. I was in demand, I was adored and cherished, and my successes were the best revenge I could ever imagine to sting my sisters over and over again, tormenting them with the venom of my popularity and status and making their lives miserable."

After her compelling and passionate disclosure, Lily paused, and her genuineness, like an electric impulse, felt throughout my body. I needed time to absorb everything I heard from Lily because I started feeling lightheaded and even tired. At the same time, I did not want to stop her and knew she needed to speak up as much as I needed to listen to her. So, we both took a deep breath, and I asked her what else happened. "My fame among rich and influential people who attended my bewitching performances in my father's theater grew with me, and my lust for power and wealth grew even faster. After each performance, I was surrounded by admirers who wanted my attention and an intimate relationship with me, and I was a willing participant in such an exchange of services. When I became old enough with my fame and wealth, I moved into one of the most luxurious houses in Saint-Petersburg and was never alone. My life consisted of never-stopping adventures, performances, attractions, and flirting. My irresistible charms like ambers from a firework ignited more and more flames and affections, thus corralling more esteemed people into my circle of influence.

I thought this life would last forever, but I became sick one day while traveling with my father's theater and started coughing. At first, I did not give much attention to this cough and continued with the same busy schedule of my performances and parties with passionate nights afterward. But my body was not willing to be neglected anymore, and instead of getting better, my cough quickly worsened, and when I saw the first drops of blood on my handkerchief, I knew what it meant. My family doctor, who treated me since I was a child, told me about tuberculosis and gave me an ultimatum. He said that I could move to a warmer climate to treat and heal my lungs because staying in Saint-Petersburg would lead to my premature demise.

That night I was alone for the first time in a long time and looked back, taking an honest assessment of my life. I did not cry nor felt sorry for myself. I prayed hard and asked for guidance and forgiveness. Praying, I fell asleep, and when I woke up, it was clear to me that I will remain in my home and not be running to a warmer climate to save myself. I lived a glorious life; I did what I wanted, how I wanted, and when I wanted. My life was adventurous and even exciting, and I had no regrets how it all turned out. The only regret I could name was that I created (or built) my life on the foundation of revenge, I felt toward my older sisters, and all the fame and success I reached was out of spite and not because I was so inspired to do so.

Yet, in the end, who cares? One way or another, I accomplished my goals, and when my time comes, I will be ready to depart, with peace in my heart and love for the roles I played my whole life. The memory of me and my talents will be long-lived in the theater, and my sisters would not be able to erase it."

I asked Lily if she ever regretted not falling in love with someone special, not birthing children, and having a family. Lily was adamant about her choices and said that the life I described was never for her. She said she was destined to become a star, and having family and having children was against any of her dreams and desires. She was a social butterfly, and she desired to dazzle, sparkle, and radiate her light, not live a dimmed life.

Lily said that once she decided to stay, even her illness improved for a short time, but then fast, like a snowball, went downhill.

"My last days I spent with my favorite brother Andrew, who I adored and loved all my life and looked up to. He knew about my lifestyle, but he never judged me, never criticized me, and just loved me for who I was, his baby sister. He was with me when I took my last breath, and he closed my eyes. By then, both of my parents departed, and they did not know that I died so young. Andrew was a director of our family theater, with our sisters working there and helping him. As strange as it sounds, I am actually grateful to my sisters for helping me grow that thick skin, thus preparing me for life to handle anything."

I asked Lily if she felt the need to forgive herself or her sisters or any of her relationships, but she declined my offer and said it sounded awkward. "Why would I forgive myself? For what? You, Alla, are very strange, asking me this stupid question. What I did brightened up people's lives and made them feel better, more loved, more accepted, and sometimes even more famous. Maybe some could call my lifestyle a prostitute, but the description of my services was so positive and so highly acclaimed that it did not define me. "

At that moment, I decided that asking more questions after such a riveting confession would not be helpful, moreover, unnecessary.

I apologized to Lily for the years of carrying judgments against her and said how appreciative I was for her openness, willingness to set the record straight, and playing such a role in my awakening. Lily smiled and sighed. She thanked me for having the courage to seek answers, not being ordinary, and finding my ways to be different. Lily looked at me and asked: "Now you know why you have lung issues this time around?"

Her question about my current breathing condition indicated that I carried on the cell memory of her terminal illness into this life and manifested as twice having pneumonia and subsequently chronic breathing issues.

I now know how essential it was to dissect Lily's life regardless of my resistance and self-imposed obstacles.

Besides understanding the connection of her terminal illness to my current lung challenges, I also see how her strong personality, her desire to succeed, and forcefulness became parts of my character and psychological makeup. The exploration into this life reminded me of a lesson I learned years ago but ignored in practice: "NEVER ASSUME." My assumptions about that lifetime were unwarranted, uncalled for, and unhealthy. I am grateful that by writing this chapter, I shifted my perception from "bitter to better" and became a bigger person in the process of this healing journey.

And So It Is.

CHAPTER 13

"At the solemn moment of death, every man, even when death is sudden, sees the whole of his past life marshalled before him, in its minutest details. For one short instant the personal becomes one with the individual and all-knowing ego. But this instant is enough to show to him the whole chain of causes which have been at work during his life."
— **Annie Besant**

Death in the Dungeon

The vague memory of yet another life came to my awareness in Sedona. In 2005 I began attending a yoga center in my neighborhood, and sometime later, I surprisingly met my former classmate Barbara who also joined the center. Barbara and I knew each other back in the nineties; we were both students at the Hypnosis Motivation Institute in Tarzana in 1996-1997. We learned hypnotherapy techniques to assist ourselves and others in their transformation and healing. Since then, we've been friends. A couple of years into our attendance at the yoga center, the yoga master announced that our center was organizing a meditation retreat in Sedona. We decided it would be good to take this opportunity, deepen our yoga and meditation practice, travel to Sedona together, and be roommates.

The retreat was even more than we anticipated; everything was flawless, the grounds of the center, the lake, the meals, the caring and pleasant staff- everything was high quality and high energy.

The only thing that clouded my fabulous personal experiences was the breathing issue that made my stay there challenging.

One evening after our dinner, when I was especially gasping for air, Barbara (an excellent masseuse that knew other energy work modalities) said she could do energy work to help me breathe easier.

I instantly agreed to such an offer in hopes of stopping feeling suffocated. While Barbara was working with energies, I closed my eyes and followed her suggestion to relax and envision where I was when I could not breathe and what else had happened. After hearing these words, I suddenly felt that I was in complete darkness, the air was cold, and the walls of that place were wet and slimy. It was hard to breathe and see anything around me, and I felt how my body was shivering from the hair-raising fear mixed with the bone-chilling dampness.

I had no idea how my mind (or what?) flipped to that place in a flash. I told Barbara that I was a young male in France, dressed in exquisite but worn-out, even ripped clothes, from being thrown into this terrible place. I said that it was a dungeon, and I could not breathe. No other information came to me while I was getting energy treatment from Barbara. She continued to work on moving my energy until I fell asleep. When I woke up later that night, my breathing stabilized, and I was happy that she helped me "catch a breath," and I didn't have to think about breathing for the rest of my stay there.

From time to time, when my breathing became difficult again, and the familiar feeling of suffocation came back, the image of that young male dying in a dungeon would surface in my memory to remind me of the vision I had in Sedona.

However, up until now, as it happened with exploring other past lives, I was not in a hurry to delve into the story of this life because what I had a glimpse of in Sedona was so disturbing and grim that traumatizing me by invoking that memory did not seem helpful. I had suspicions that the breathing challenges I faced since my early twenties could have their origins with that young male and what happened to him in that dark and frightening chamber. Dying from suffocation left its toxic imprint on his cell memory. Whether someone choked him to death or he died in an oxygen-deprived torture chamber mattered somewhat, but what was important is that the memory of the moment of his death was transferred with its inability to breathe and became a chronic issue for me for years.

In one of Sylvia Browne's books, I read that our issues, whether health or other, may originate from how and when one of our previous lives ended. Of course, I realize that this concept sounds a little mystical. "It sounds too bizarre," you may say; "how is this even possible?" But as impossible as it may sound to you, it rings true to me because, in my view, it is not an accident that the age of this young male's demise coincided with the time in my early twenties when normal breathing became a big challenge for me.

When I started thinking and working on this chapter, my intent to connect with this young male grew stronger. I knew nothing of him before the moment of his death in the torture chamber. Now I wanted to know about him before his end in that dungeon; his name, who he was, what were his dreams and aspirations. How do I approach him, I was asking myself? The last thing I wanted to do is to disturb or offend him by asking him to come forward and speak of his life before his last minutes on earth. All these thoughts were disconcerting to me. What do I gain by doing this? Would the information be helpful or harmful? The answer came when I remembered that assuming something was not a good idea and the lesson I learned while writing the previous chapter. Never Assume.

All the information came to me very swiftly, as a sudden download. One day, with the bits of information I had about him, and my intent to do no harm, I quieted my mind and brought the image of the dungeon I saw in Sedona. I asked the young male to speak to me. Right before I saw him before my closed eyes, I felt familiar goosebumps in my body. As if on a screen, he appeared in his richly made clothes, but they were not ripped or damaged. He looked different too and did not seem hurt. I immediately felt emotional relief because, gratefully, he was not the same as the image I held for all these years. I greeted him thankfully, telling him the reason for calling him forth. I asked for his name and his story.

"My name is Jacques, he said. "I was born in France after the French Revolution. My family suffered because they belonged to the royal family but fortunately survived the horrors of those violent and unpredictable times. I was the youngest and the only surviving child in a family when I was born. My older brothers and sisters all died before and during the revolution. The times were hard even for royalty, and my parents could not protect their brood from illnesses and lack of doctor's care. My mother told me that her children were sickly and frail, and my parents could not save them from dying at such young ages.

I grew up in a loving family, adored by my parents, especially my mother; she treated me like a precious gift because they did not expect more children. My mother taught me arts and music; I played musical instruments and even composed a little. Nothing special, but my small successes made my mother swell with pride and joy for me. My father wanted to toughen me up, to raise me to be fearless and daring. Still, my mother shielded me from any chivalrous actions she deemed unsafe, and I, reacting to her motherly love, shied away from dangerous, in her view, games and strenuous activities.

Although I lived in a bubble created by my adoring mother, who wished to protect and spoil me at every turn while growing up, I intuitively knew that living such a sheltered life was no longer suitable when I reached young adulthood. To please my mother, I continued to compose music and practice musical instruments and even wrote an opera to honor my brothers and sisters to the amusement and joy of my mother. She even hired a musical director who gathered actors in our palace, and with his help, they performed the opera for our many guests. Unfortunately, to the disappointment of my loving mother, that opera never became popular and was only performed once. I remembered that the guests were politely cheering the actors, and some whispered that they liked the music, but overall, it was a flop. But even this fiasco did not discourage my devoted mother enough, and she continued to dream and hope that one day I will become renowned and famous, and the music I will compose will become classic.

After I turned 19 years old, my father called me one day to his study. It did not happen often, and I felt a little apprehensive about his unusual move. However, my father appeared serious, and I thought I might have done something wrong; that's why he was angry at me. But my father was not mad at me. Instead, he sat me on one of the intricate chairs placed around his desk, and in his calm and caring voice, he told me how much he loved my musical talents, my abilities to play instruments, and the music I composed. He praised me and said the time had come to get serious and start training in martial arts and military games. My father said that he would keep it a secret and he would not tell my mother about my new studies so that she would not get worried or concerned about me getting hurt. My father said he would think of an excuse to get me out of the palace to train in martial arts.

My father decided this for me, without leaving me a choice to either agree or disagree. It was a done deal in his mind, and now it was just a matter of finding under what reason I could leave the palace. I had mixed feelings over my father's authoritarian decision to know what was better for me and make me someone I was not or did not want to become. I was concerned about how concealing the truth from my mother would make me dishonest and dishonorable. It was a bitter pill for me to swallow because of the deep love and reverence I always felt for her; she was my biggest supporter in life and my guardian angel, and lying to her was against my values.

At the same time as I was agonizing over the plausible explanation of my absences from the palace, my mother suddenly fell ill. It was so devastating to see her unable to walk or speak, becoming incapacitated so quickly. So many thoughts crawled into my mind, and one of them was that she fell ill to keep me near herself, to sacrifice herself, to keep me away from harm. Of course, I knew it was not true, but I could not come up with any other explanation of her out-of-the-blue illness. I stayed by her bed, praying and hoping she would recover soon. Unfortunately, one of the doctors in the palace my mother trusted and was fond of came to see her immediately after she fell ill and did not have any encouraging promises for my father and me. He ordered a nurse to stay by her constantly and call him if there were any changes for the worse. He said not to feed her because she could not swallow anymore but to put drops of water on her lips. I was devastated. My father was beside himself.

Along with me, he did not leave her bed, quietly sobbing, knowing the end was near. From the very little he told me during these hardest hours of my life, I understood that in the past, when his children, their children, one by one, had died of different reasons, he had to be strong to support my mother. Every death (there were four children before me) caused her more and more heartbreak, and he was always by her side to wall her off from so much loss and despair."

Jacques stopped. The pause was long. He was overwhelmed with grief; his sadness was so palpable that I felt deep compassion for him. He genuinely loved his mother, and even after over two hundred years since they both walked on this earth, it was clear and moving. Bringing up feelings of his loss and sharing them with me was incredibly healing for him. How did I know, you may ask? Because of the tension I sensed in my body when he was speaking, and how I gradually felt it less and less, releasing it with a big sigh.

I asked Jacques what had happened next, and after thinking for a second, he continued. "What else can I add to this?" he asked.

"We lost my mother the same night; she only acknowledged her passing when a single tear rolled off of her left eye. She was saying goodbye to us, I whispered to my father. He saw the tear; he was intensely looking at her or through her, probably seeing something I could not see. When her heart stopped, and my father tenderly touched her face and beautiful grey eyes, closing them forever, I realized how dearly he loved my mother, even though he never showed any affection toward her. I did not even know if my mother knew his love for her.

The loss of her children weakened her heart, yet she kept all her strength together to raise me and give me the best upbringing and her love. Seeing me grown and become successful (in her view) did not mend all the wounds and scars left on her heart, and she finally gave up her struggle. I never even knew she had heart problems, and only our palace doctor told my father later that he had been treating her heart condition for several years.

With my dear mother gone, I no longer needed an excuse to leave our palace, and after some time, I began leaving home more often and then almost daily. My father did not forget his decision to train me to become fiercer and more resilient to adversities that our society was still afflicted with years after the French Revolution. Once I got a taste of martial arts and games, I started training more often, but my body was not prepared for tough challenges, and I struggled, keeping up the pace of my exercises.

My father, meanwhile, was becoming unhappier and more agitated. It was hard for me to be around him, and though I knew he was missing my mother, I was missing her too, but I was not lashing out my pain onto others, such as our servants, for instance. Sometimes, I felt that I lost both parents because my father became distant and isolated himself from everyone, and my life in the palace became uncomfortable and depressing. I had no desire to compose or play musical instruments, and the palace without my mother became silent like a grave.

A few times, I saw strange-looking people, not from our circle of association or acquaintances. I was concerned, and once I told my father about suspicious people near our palace. My father angrily glanced at me and suggested I stay out of his business and do what he was expected of me, studying martial arts and becoming more robust. My encounter with him left me feeling uneasy and even fearful. The more I tried to dismiss my anxious thoughts, the more persistent they were, swarming like hornets stinging with their venom of dread my impressionable psyche. I was concerned about my father and his unusual associations, but I was even more concerned about my own life and survival. And based on what happened next, my fears were valid.

One day coming to the palace later at night, the carriage I was in was attacked by strangers, and I was kidnapped. Somebody rudely covered my eyes and mouth; I could not see anything or scream for help. My hands were tied too. I felt they threw me into another carriage like a bag going to market. My mind was racing, it was not a game, and I could not use any martial arts moves I had barely started to learn. The carriage stopped, and I was pulled out of it. Whoever was dragging me was very aggressive and angry, but everything he was doing, he did without making a sound or saying a word."

Jacques made another long pause, and it was evident how hard it was for him to tell me all these painful details of his brutal kidnapping. I took a deep breath myself because I was getting exhausted and depleted. I wanted him to stop, but he continued.

"I felt that two people violently picked me up by my legs and arms and threw me on the ground, hastily walking away. I heard their footsteps but could not see anything. After my initial shock and terror, I started thinking about what happened to me. I was in a dungeon, locked there, possibly forever. No one would ever know where I was and what happened to me. Somehow, I knew that I was there because of my father's enemies who grabbed, kidnapped, and forced me into this dark place to get revenge against him. Whoever these enemies were, they wanted to inflict pain on him by holding me as their prisoner and making me disappear. I was an innocent victim in the game of some influential people; I did not know why they tried to destroy my father. Even though he and I had become distant since my mother's death, I know he wanted to protect me from his dealings and intrigues by never letting me in on any of his matters. Unfortunately, I did not know how to help myself and free myself out of this dungeon."

"Days and nights were the same," he continued. "I could barely see the glimpses of light in the cracks of the thick, cobble-stone wall that was around me. With each passing moment of my tormented existence, I was getting frailer. I could no longer breathe because of the toxic, disgusting smells and the stinky cold air coming out from everywhere in the dungeon. I had no strength to scream, yell or call for help; no one could hear me. I rolled into a ball to keep a little warmth and wished death upon myself. Any tiny hope of my powerful father rescuing me was short-lived, and I knew the end of my affluent life in the royal family was almost over. Another attempt to catch my last breath failed, and I died with my breath inside because my brain, mind, and heart could no longer support this life. This misery had to end, and along with my life, my mother's dreams of me one day becoming a famous and successful composer and my father's dreams for me of becoming formidable and strong. When I was dying, I opened my eyes and saw my mother standing near me. I immediately felt the warmth of her presence and the feeling of unconditional love she imbued on me. Maybe I was hallucinating, or perhaps she took my hand and walked with me toward the enormous sun that immediately warmed up my freezing body, pouring into my heart and body feelings of tranquility and overwhelming peace." Jacques smiled. "My life ended here, not when I suffocated in the dungeon, but when I walked with my mother peacefully, warmed-up, and renewed."

I took the deepest and longest breath after such intense recollection of this past life. But there was still more to do to completely heal this memory for him and me. First of all, I thanked him immensely for opening up his life to me and sharing what he was willing to share—his memories. It was so profound and transformational for me, and I told him this. I asked him if he had any judgments over what happened, he did not seem to have any. He said that retelling his life story to me was the most cathartic moment, and he now understood why I called him forth to speak of his life. "I can see how essential what you are doing is by collecting, exploring, and dissecting each life you remembered," Jacques said. "By shining light on each of your soul's incarnations and expressing your sincere affection and interest in what happened in any of the lives, you are showing us respect, no matter how ordinary or mundane these lives were. We all were separate beings, separated by centuries, yet, linked to one another by the same powerful energy of one soul; and each of our lives, including yours, reflects its beauty and its magnificence. I am very grateful for your diligence, curiosity, and wisdom when you decided to follow up on your guidance and intuition, connected us, and helped us reclaim and heal the memories of our lives."

When Jacques finished speaking on behalf of past lives that came forward for healing, I felt complete. I was grateful when Jacques said his life ended when he walked toward the sun with his mother, not when he died from suffocation and fear. It was vital for me to know because it gave me the tool to stop reacting to my breathing problem once and for all. I decided that if I start gasping for air, I can see Jacques and his mother walking toward the sun, and just fixing this image on my mind's screen will bring calming effects and stop the shortness of breath.

And So It Is.

CHAPTER 14

"When a person who has had highly evolved past lives is going through a strong past-life transit, that person comes to know things about life, death and other dimensions that most people in our world aren't aware of."
— Frederick Lenz

High Priestess

As I conclude this book of my past lives, I am aware of at least one more life that I want to look at and explore, even though I do not have personal memory or experience of this life. How did I find out about this life, then? I think it would be an appropriate question.

In the story of The Scribe, I already mentioned that several years ago, one of my friends, Barbara, told me in one of our conversations about two lifetimes she and I had together. She said that she remembered us in Ancient Egypt as High Priestess, serving a Pharaoh, and buried alive with Pharaoh after his death. Although Nina and I were seemingly worlds apart, coming to the US from different countries and backgrounds, we, nonetheless, had many things in common; we had similar interests and beliefs in spirituality, self-development, and everything associated with it. We were also interested in reincarnations and past lives and often discussed books we read on this subject. We attended many seminars together, she introduced me to concepts in spiritual development I did not know before, and we always had interesting discussions together. So, hearing this revelation from her was not too shocking; moreover, what she said made sense to me because of our commonality. That is why I did not even question what she said, just memorized and put it on a "back burner" until now.

I know now that writing about this life will be different because its memory was not mine. When I asked Nina if she remembered anything else, she said no; she just knew of our connection to ancient Egypt and that we were High Priestesses. She said we were buried together with a Pharaoh when he died as part of his entourage. That was it. I knew I needed to find the "rest of the story." My story. And yet, I had to rely on Nina's hypothesis, tapping into the life in Ancient Egypt without any recollection of it. At least to explore the possibility that it might have happened and I had a life as a High Priestess in ancient Egypt worth digging into.

Where do I start, and what clues do I have for such an investigation? I was curious where it would take me and what I could uncover. I looked back at my other stories to see if there was any common thread and noticed that it was and it happened to be connected to my physical body. Obviously. There was no known physical body connection in this case, so I needed to look for other ways to "connect the dots."

And looking for these "dots" began with my interests related to Ancient Egypt and its associations. The first "dot" was my strong interest in Tarot cards. Tarot cards and Ancient Egypt? The common knowledge is that the first Tarot decks came from Europe sometime in the Middle Ages, but other discoveries linked them to Ancient Egypt.

When I received my very first deck as a gift many years ago, I was in awe of the cards. By now, I probably own 12-15 different decks of Tarot cards, but that first one, like first love, forever captured my heart. And my favorite card of the deck is the High Priestess. Since that first deck of cards, I always felt an affinity to the High Priestess card, even identifying myself with its image. So what? You may ask. Big deal! Many card readers love this card; it's just a beautiful card depicting a beautiful woman. And I would agree with your argument. And yet, every time I pulled this card, I felt connected with the High Priestess. I know this is a lame reason, and it does not mean much.

Another "dot" was my interest in ancient Egypt since I was a schoolgirl. I remembered my fascination in history class to learn about ancient Egypt, its culture, traditions, and beliefs. I was shocked by the cruelty of their rule relating to a Pharaoh and what happened after his death. Because in Ancient Egypt, they believe in the eternal life of their Pharaohs. After their death, everyone who served them had to die either forcefully or voluntarily by drinking poison so that they could continue to assist him in eternal life. I remember my history teacher saying that it was considered a big honor for the servants to follow a Pharaoh and die this way, but it sounded too cruel to me, the Soviet schoolgirl.

Later, I learned that not everyone was dead at the burial. Some, for whatever reason, remained alive at the moment of the tomb closing and died later. That made me question if I was one of those buried alive.

Maybe I was, and if it was so, then I no longer wondered why that life did not leave any memory, unlike others. I think that the severe psychological trauma of such an ending blocked its recollection. Do you remember the book with stuck-together pages from my long-ago dream? The book of my past lives from which it all began? What if one of these pages was about that life? I guess until I delve into that life's story, I would not know.

Goosebumps immediately covered my body as soon as I finished the last sentence as if my body was saying to me, "yes, you are on the right path, come on, step in, and let's find out together. You are safe now, so no matter what you unearth, you are not in any harm. Look at all previous revelations and everything that you uncovered up until now."

After hearing this encouraging voice inside my head, I thought I was ready to begin. But was I? I felt a block inside that prevented me from seeing anything. What was blocking me? Was it that door the tomb was closed with after the burial? I could not breathe either, and it was becoming physically uncomfortable for me. "Take a deep breath," I heard the same voice inside my head. I listened and took three, slow deep breaths to stabilize my breathing but still felt shortness of breath and nausea. I took three more, getting oxygen in, which made me feel lightheaded, even dizzy; then, I felt my heart drop. It created a strange sensation in my body, and I realized it was from fear. ' Fear of what? I asked.

"Of dying, of course," I heard in my head, and goosebumps covered my body as a confirmation that I was tapping into the last moments of that life. After that realization, I had to regain inner balance so that I could continue.

"You were skeptical by nature and questioned everything and everyone," the voice continued, "even when you were elected to advance to the position of High Priestess. You felt profound honor to be around Pharaoh, who you adored and worshipped, yet, you quietly questioned his godly status. The split you felt between your inner belief and the outside world created a certain conflict inside you when performing your duty and service to the Highest Authority. For you, the Highest Authority was Ra, God. And observing Pharaoh and his actions, you could not find many signs of godly conduct and attitude. You held your own for a long time; you did not share your thoughts with anybody knowing well the danger of thinking outside of group thinking. You wished Pharaoh good health, knowing that everyone around him will have to accompany him to eternal life once he is dead, and you, sure, did not want eternal life. You loved and revered this life."

Everything the voice was communicating seemed accurate, and flashes of goosebumps continued to validate what was said. " You had natural inborn abilities to heal, and your unique curative approach made you well known. Your healing skills opened the path for you to become High Priestess, and Pharaoh especially wanted you to be close to him and help him with any ailments, afflictions, or conditions he or his family could have. Out of your own desire to stay alive, you saved Pharaoh's life from at least three attempts to poison him. Your premonition, foresight, and genuine care for his well-being made you trustworthy, and that, in return, allowed you to alert him when he was about to be in danger.

Because of your devotion, bravery, and selfless (or so it seemed) service to Pharaoh, you were cherished and protected from others because your special status provoked envy and hidden hostility toward you. However, it was not unknown to you; you could read and understand people's thoughts, motives and actions well in advance, and you were several steps ahead of those who dreamed you harm."

The voice in my head was getting more intense and what was said captivated me completely. I was not even asking questions about the Priestess or anything else; the information was downloading, seemingly without my participation. Even more interesting, the voice was speaking to her (i.e., High Priestess), not to me; I was more of an observer, listening and recording the narration. I did not want to interrupt this moment, closed my eyes, and continued listening, but the moment had ended, and the voice spoke to me. " You are marveling about me and my role in the life of the High Priestess. I am her Life Force, her Higher Self. She had a powerful connection to me from her birth, and that connection allowed her to know things others never did. It was her most important gift, talent, virtue. She was clairvoyant, psychically open; she had expanded awareness of not only what was seen but also to the unseen, extraterrestrial world. Her abilities to hear me and interpret my messages were unique and masterful. She was special in so many ways, and her inner beauty matched her outer beauty; she had large dark eyes, shiny-black long hair, tall, straight and gorgeous stature."

After this introduction by the Higher Self, I wanted to get to know the High Priestess and see if I could draw any parallels between our lives. I asked her Higher Self permission to approach the High Priestess, realizing that her noble status in ancient society still matters and requires respect and even reverence. I felt a slight nod from her Higher Self and received approval to speak to her. In my mind, I pictured a tall, dark-haired woman with a headdress that made her even taller. I needed no introduction or reason for my inquiry; I felt as if her elongated eyes looked directly into my heart, reading something in the language only she knew. Her face moved, possibly mimicking a smile, and I smiled back. There was a tension that made me question whether my decision to dig into this life was right. She immediately responded to me without me saying a word: " Don't question your decision to connect with me; you were right to follow your intuition. I have much to share with you and teach you about yourself, so don't doubt your inclination. I know what you want from me, but there is so much more that you have no knowledge of and would not even know to ask me." I just nodded my head in agreement and prepared to listen.

"First of all, let me tell you my name because you call me High Priestess, and it is okay, but I have a name, and I want to be known by my name. I am Raia, and was named to honor, celebrate, and exalt Ra, our God. My family belonged to an upper class, but not close to the Pharaoh's dynasty. One of the servants in my family, who my mother trusted with raising me, noticed my unusual gift of clairvoyance and prediction from an early age. When I was old enough to be separated from my mother, my parents proudly sent me to school, where I studied to become Junior Priestess. The studies helped me build on my rich innate foundation, and I quickly became one of the best students in the academy. The accuracy with which I predicted events and details in advance made my teachers swell with pride of my incredible abilities, and at the same time to be concerned for me because I could become a threat to someone influential and powerful. I was told to never speak up until or unless I was asked specific information about something. Or someone. I felt that it could hold me back, and my natural openness and naivety wanted to share and help others if I could. However, my teachers were adamant about keeping my prophetic abilities to myself unless Pharaoh called me to give him the information he needed or wanted from me.

It was a Divinity school where I studied healing arts, magic, and rituals to perform in the Temple. Even though I was very accurate in prophesying future events, I learned one of the most amazing tools to help me become an even more prophetic and enlightened healer. One of my favorite teachers introduced me to Thoth's Cards. He taught me to read Thoth's cards with images that sparked my imagination and greatly expanded my storytelling skills. From the moment I saw the deck, I was in awe, and ever since, they became my best friends because of the secrets they shared with me. I also could ask them anything, and they would never lie to me. This teacher gifted me a deck containing magic colors, through which I learned to connect with Higher Realms. I studied the cards faithfully, and the more I got to know them, the more secrets and mysteries the cards opened for me. My diligence and tenacity paid off, and soon I became the most prolific Priestess.

My fame opened the door for me to the Temple that served Pharaoh and his family dynasty. My parents were ecstatic to know that my talents were noticed, and their pride was immense. In the Temple where I served God Ra, I performed rituals to please Ra with prayers and actions. Having profound healing skills helped me heal and rejuvenate others, bring them back to health, give them medicinal herbs, and apply energetic healing. Because I wanted to serve more people, I, sometimes with my aide, dressed very modestly not to be recognized and just came to a smaller temple to heal and teach others. My cards were always with me, and I often sought guidance from them, tapping into their wisdom, seeking answers sometimes for myself, primarily for others."

"Can you please tell me more about the rituals, magic, and healing you performed in a Temple," I asked her; please tell me more, "It was my best service at the time I went to a smaller Temple to heal and help ordinary people. The Priest in that Temple knew me well, but he never revealed my secret from where I came, and it allowed me to use my many skills,' Raia said.

"I had people waiting for me to heal them, but I was especially effective in healing and restoring children if they had injuries. Their mothers trusted me, and their faith in me and my abilities gave me even more power to heal. One day mother brought a boy who hit his head, falling from a roof and screaming from pain. Gladly I was there that time, and I immediately attended to him. I diagnosed his head energetically, moving my hands around his body, stabilizing his neck, and reducing his pain by holding his head with my hands. At that moment, I was guided to check his neck and realized his neck was fractured. Poor child, I thought. I called my aide to hold his head so as not to let him move while I reassembled all small bones and joints on his neck, sealing his injury with a cast. The Priest was giving the boy drops of herbal tea to help the child with pain. The mother of this poor boy was crying and moaning, seeing her child in such distress, and I offered her another medicinal tea to calm her. Once the child stopped crying and sobbing, I knew that I healed his neck; he was on the way to recovery and will get well."

She continued: "Another day, a young woman came to me to ask about her sister, saying she was afraid of her and thought her sister wanted to harm her. I invited her to a small enclosure where she could openly speak. Her voice was trembling, her words expressed fear, and her eyes were wide open and filled with sheer terror. She spoke of the animosity her sister developed toward her, this sweet and pretty young woman. I reached to get the Thoth's cards, gently tapping on them, as if I called forth their Spirit, inwardly praying for their guidance. When I opened the cards, the images validated the fears and terror of this young woman. Her intuitive sense warned about her wicked sister and sister's evil plans to harm and get rid of that young woman. The cards told me a story of extreme envy of the older sister and gave the young woman the warning to sleep with one eye open. The cards showed me that the wicked sister might try to harm this young woman, but not worry because the sister won't succeed. Moreover, the sister will soon disappear from the home and won't come back. I taught her prayers and simple rituals for protection, and the young woman left in peace."

Raia enjoyed telling me her stories, her examples of care and compassion for others, and her desire to help those who could not pay but could always donate to Temple. She encouraged people to do such acts of kindness. "I would love you to tell me more about the Pharaoh's Temple and what rituals and magic you performed there," I asked her. She said that her duty consisted of routine actions to glorify and communicate with the gods, worship Pharaoh, and the whole dynasty. "My communication with the gods was secretive and was only to be shared with Pharaoh. Then he was deciding who else to speak to disseminate the information if it was appropriate. I knew that the accuracy of the messages I received from communication with the gods was essential because everything depended on it: wars, harvests, health, lives, and so much more. And I always strived to deliver the best possible information.

However, I could not use Thoth cards or heal others when in Pharaoh's Temple; it was not appropriate for a High Priestess to engage in these activities. But when I went to a small Temple for ordinary people, I opened my heart to others, helped children heal, taught parents to care for their ill children, and used my cards to answer their questions. This is what made my life meaningful and my skills needed.

One day in my communication with the gods, they told me that our Pharaoh is coming down with a disease that will end his life. The gods told me to speak to Pharaoh directly and tell him what they said. I immediately performed a ritual praying for wisdom and strength in approaching Pharaoh with such unwelcome news and inwardly prepared myself for this. I felt as if a dust storm took over inside me, with many different emotions from fear to anger, from sadness to sorrow stirred up the wind and knocked me over. It was a first for me, I never had to be a messenger of such news, but deep inside, I knew that such a message would come one day.

I had to prepare myself before such a meeting. In the past, I delivered various messages to the Pharaoh, and I used to communicate to him the gods' wishes or warnings. Still, I never felt any hesitation in speaking to Pharaoh with reverence and adoration. Now it was different. By the time I faced the Pharaoh, my composure was back, and, looking him straight in the eyes, I delivered the message from the gods. The gods did not tell me how much time the Pharaoh has in this life, which was the first question he asked me. I bowed my head in respect and replied that it was not foretold. I felt his upset, though he could not express it in front of me.

He allowed me to leave, knowing that I could not tell him more than I already said. After a short pause, the Pharaoh asked me to keep this a secret so that no one could use this knowledge to kill him or harm his family. I again bowed my head in agreement and left him standing in the middle of his big hall.

I knew what was coming next for me and for all who were serving him. However, bound by the oath to keep a secret, I had to be silent. Every morning, my prayers and rituals became even more fervent because I was pleading with the gods to spare the Pharaoh life so that my life could be saved too. The Pharaoh, meanwhile, announced a huge gathering and invited many guests from far and near places to celebrate with him.

Sensing that his departure nears, and knowing that I, as one a High Priestess and his confidant, will be sent with him and others on the journey to the eternal life, I increased my visits to the small Temple so that I could heal and help more, while I was still in my physical body. ". Raia stopped her incredible story, and what she was saying became dramatic and emotional for me.

I felt that the story was coming to an end and stayed quiet.

I think she appreciated my listening and continued.

"Not long after the Pharaoh's celebration gathering, he was sitting with his advisors, when he suddenly fell ill and slid off the chair, falling on the floor, hitting his head. It happened so fast that no one could even react and stop him from falling. He was taken to his quarters, unconscious, pale, and lifeless. His family surrounded him, and his wife and mother started crying, understanding that they would go with him. His children were to stay, and one of his sons was going to become the next Pharaoh.

Once the Pharaoh's soul left his lifeless body, the servants started preparing his body for traveling. We all accompanied his body to the tomb, and then each of us was given a small glass bottle of the poison to leave painlessly. All of us, including his wife and mother, obediently did what we were told and sat around the Pharaoh's mummified body. I closed my eyes; the gods appeared before me and reassured me that I don't have to worry. I was still alive when I heard someone sobbing, grieving their lost lives. I then fell into a deep sleep, thinking that my life was over. And I have to tell you, it would be such a grand finale to exit this way, but it was not the end. Somehow, I survived. The poison did not kill me completely, and I woke up feeling sick, nauseous, and terrified. When I regained full consciousness and realized that I was alone, I bawled my eyes out. Probably from my loud crying and sobbing, someone else awoke, and I heard a weak squeak coming from my left. I got up, my feet shaking and feeling dizzy; I unsteadily walked to where the soft voice came. I saw another High Priestess who shared my fate of not dying after poison. We cried together, still not believing that we were now among the dead, but we seemed alive. After sufficient crying, we started looking for an exit, but everything was sealed. Then we knew that we had no chance of ever seeing the Sun again, and we decided to die together. We walked around dead bodies, collecting every bottle that was dropped near them so that we could drink what was left over to do it again. Luckily, it was enough for both of us, and this time we wanted to die. With each moment, staying alive in this horrible, air and light-deprived tomb was becoming impossible. No wonder I was skeptical from an early age about many things. And I found out the story of eternal life was a big lie that led to so many unnecessary deaths, innocent souls sacrificed for something that never happened and never will. We were ready to leave this time for real. Holding bottles in one hand and holding each other, we closed our eyes, each said a small prayer, and this time we died quickly.

I did not want to; I could not interrupt that long silence after the tragically sad story of her extraordinary life was over.

As I was listening to her, throughout her long story, my body was generously reacting to many moments by flashes of goosebumps, validating Barbara's memory. I knew that the High Priestess that died with me the second time was Barbara. Our bond of dying together survived millennia, and this time we were placed into each other's lives, actually to become friends. And we did.

I did not feel a need to ask Raia any questions; I think I heard enough to accept her life as one of mine and include it in my book.

As I am concluding this chapter, I know that the High Priestess captivated my mind, my heart, and from now on, her presence in my current life will be permanent. I am aware that she is now a significant part of me, and I am eternally grateful.

And So It Is.

"The Soul which is approaching its' liberation, as it looks back over past lives... down the vistas of the centuries along which it has slowly been climbing.

... is able to see there the way in which the bonds were made, the causes which set it in motion. It is able to see how many of those causes have worked themselves out and... how many... are still working themselves out."
— **Annie Besant**

The End is Only the Beginning

Now, as my book is coming to an end and some of my past lifetimes revealed themselves to me through meditations, regressions, or writing, I realize how important it was to give myself permission to write and bring this book to fruition. I believe that dream about the famous book of my past lives my husband made for me has many more pages than I uncovered thus far. I intend to continue exploring, connecting the dots between past and present, discovering other lives, and healing their memories.

Writing this book became a grand experiment for me, and every time I began a new chapter, I only had one intention: to be open. I was open to whatever might show up in my consciousness rising from the Great Unknown, ready to become known. My first journey through lifetimes, being different people with different stories, is winding out, and I am grateful and honored that you have decided to stick with me to the end. My gratitude is to you, my reader, that you are still with me, letting your imagination and curiosity travel along.

And I hope that in this buffet of experiences that you just read about, you found something that triggered your memory or your curiosity and made you ask a question or two.

When I decided to write this book, I had no way of knowing where this "unearthing of graves" would take me. The information I could rely on was scarce, whether it was a picture from the dream or a physical sensation as a starting point, whether it was a skin rash, chronic back pain, or chronic shortness of breath. These and other physical symptoms troubled me on and off, patiently waiting for my awakening for when I become aware and curious enough, wanting to explore and understand these issues on a deeper level. I intuitively felt that knowing this information could be a key to my healing. And my continual desire to find ways and get healed led me, like North Star, to pursue new things, learn, explore, and experiment, thus raising the bar for more quests.

My quest for healing myself did not originate from a deficit of medical professionals, whether in the former Soviet Union or the United States. I always sought help from doctors first, exhausting all possible avenues, following medical advice, hoping that this next doctor will be the one that would magically take my woes away. My burning desire to live in a pain-free body remained unfulfilled year after year, and time only added new unsuccessfully treated conditions to the list.

There is no need to bore you with my health challenges, but be certain that I attempted and tried many things, only to get disappointed by the lack of results. I then moved to alternative healings in high hopes that it would finally bring me the relief and subsequent improvement I so desired. Although I did get some help here and there, and some treatments were more beneficial than others (like crystal therapy or homeopathy, for example,) my overall condition made me continue my quest for better health.

And looking back, I was thankful that these physical challenges offered me an opportunity to become more proactive, more invested in my health, and search for solutions to improve, overcome, and get better. When I realized that my physical challenges ought to be rooted not in a physical body, I stepped on a spiritual path, a path of spiritual development and spiritual growth, which ultimately led me to look to my past lives.

When I started this last part of the book, I thought reading all the chapters first would help tie the ends and prepare this book for "landing." Doing this was very useful because some of the chapters I wrote almost two years ago, and I needed to refresh my memory and re-connect with them again. After I completed reading all chapters, my intuition suggested connecting with the Essence or Spirit of my book and listen to what it has to say. By now (I hope), you are less surprised about some strange techniques I use to receive the information. Moreover, you may even like some of them, and in the future, you may want to try them too.

Following this brilliant intuition, I attuned to the book's essence and was pleasantly surprised by the information I received. When I asked questions, the answers started pouring in. The Book Essence said that it appreciated the respect and attention it received.

This admission was unexpected and comforting at the same time. TBE (short for The Book Essence) told me that this book and all others I write in the future would impact and raise human consciousness, thus fulfilling my life purpose. As strange as it was, I felt like I received mentoring from my book because it suggested writing about my feelings, challenges I met, and what helped me overcome them. TBE encouraged me to look into the lessons learned and talk about how gender roles played in past lives and how my current physical health condition could relate to the distant past. I received instructions and valuable ideas on mapping out this last part of the book. It was another validation of the incredible power of Gestalt, and when it's used for guidance, it becomes a source of insight and wisdom we all possess.

After this, I felt I was getting ready to wrap it up and decided to start with the most obvious observation: I was both males and females in my past lives, playing roles of both genders, and one time it was an inanimate life. Out of 14 lives, I wrote about, seven times I was a male (a warrior, a cowboy, a monk, an immigrant boy, a scribe, a royalty, a farmer, and six lifetimes as female (the witch, the Mayan girl, the young mother, the entertainer, the poetess, and the High Priestess). Each of these lives left a mark on my cell memory for better or for worse, and each life made an impact on me, whether it's not walking barefoot or loving Tarot cards, or having a green thumb, or adopting a dog that was my horse in the past life.) The list can go on, but you got the drift. Without writing about this, I would never make such inexplicable connections.

Almost every life ended prematurely, between a 12-year-old teenager drowning in New York and possibly the oldest as a High Priestess, in her late twenties dying in Ancient Egypt. I did not know how old the cowboy was because I have not looked into his death circumstances. I noticed that out of 14 lives that I was allowed to see and present in this book, only once I had a life as a parent, a mother, but that parenthood did not last for more than a few hours before I succumbed to death, leaving my child an orphan. Another interesting observation is that in this life, I birthed my child and raised her to adulthood, basically for the first time becoming a mother and experiencing motherhood. Nothing is random in this Universe, and I believe it is not by chance that the baby girl was named Elizabeth after her mother died, and this is the same name I gave my daughter when she was born. Seriously, how can this be? Or be explained?

And how to explain that centuries later after that death from bleeding during childbirth, in this life, I was dying from bleeding during the failed tube pregnancy when my daughter was only four years old. When I was in surgery and doctors desperately tried to save my life,

I had a Near Death Experience, ready to cross over. I believe that I changed my mind to die young again and made adjustments on the Soul Level to my original plan because I could not leave my daughter an orphan again. I survived that surgery and the whole ordeal. I hope you can follow this connecting the dots moment and see the links between then and now.

Writing this last part helped me to summarize all my experiences, observations, emotions, thoughts, and feelings while immersed in this process. It was taxing on the body at times, and I even became physically ill a couple of times, pausing the writing. It was hard not to feel compassion and sadness over the circumstances in which some of the lives ended. Anxiety was my constant companion because I never knew what I was going to find out in the process of "digging the graves." I looked at many aspects of these lives, making parallels, and realized that in none of the lives presented, I was a merchant, selling something besides my service, like in a story of the witch. No wonder that I could not find a bone of a salesperson in my body in this life and always had a tough time selling. Another observation is that this is the only life when I have a long marriage. In two out of 13 lives, I was married, but not for long. I observed that I was financially well off in most of my lives, and only in the life of a teenage boy who immigrated to the United States, I came from a poor, like a church mouse family.

I also want to say a few words about so many valuable lessons learned when writing this book. And one of them is writing in a non-native language. It was a mighty goal and presented many challenges. For me, it was an act of determination and motivation to succeed, proving to myself and others that I can do it. On the other hand, writing has expanded my awareness; it was rewarding, healing, emotional, inspiring, educational, and intentional. It became evident during the writing process that as I was releasing old, deeply buried memories, I was making space for new things to come, to live in a pain-free and better-oxygenated body. Healing memories of lives in which the body suffered from physical pain helped me to reduce pains dramatically, improving the quality of my life.

I am still working on healing breathing issues, thinking that maybe other lives that remain hidden for now may hold the secrets to healing this issue.

I think I only scratched the surface of exploring these lives, and TBE told me that this part of the book is the most personal and advised me not to be afraid to be vulnerable, to open up and write from the heart without a fear to be judged. The TBE said: "You are writing this book for yourself, to yourself, about yourself and through yourself. Many will benefit from your openness and sincerity, so think of those whose lives could be changed by just reading and comparing your experiences to theirs. When the light bulb goes in your readers' heads, or they suddenly have an epiphany, they will be grateful to you for your willingness to share yourself and your experiences from your past lives."

These words from the book's wisdom inspired and encouraged me that this first book won't be the last. Like a faithful guard, this book keeps many secrets, and in due time I will be guided when to start a 'new expedition' in the time machine. I felt that there is so much more to uncover from the stuck-together pages, and there are more lives to bring to the surface and dissect. Today I am aware of and ready to explore the second past life of a High Priestess, the life in Atlantis, the life as a treasure hunter, and the life in a future time. How do I know about these lives, you may ask, and why did you not include them in this book? It is a very fair question. The knowledge about these lives came to me from external sources, like the life of the High Priestess, for example. I did not recall them; other people who did my past life readings or other psychic readings at different times told me about them. Therefore, I decided to wait until the right time to "open" more pages, learn and explore them, and the many mysteries they hide will continue as I continue turning the pages.

RECOMMENDED READING

Through Time into Healing, By Brian Weiss, M.D

Past Lives, Future Healing, By Sylvia Browne

Many Lives, Many Masters. By Brian Weiss, M.D

Only Love is Real. By Brian Weiss, M.D

Messages from the Masters. By Brian Weiss, M.D

Same Soul, Many Bodies, By Brian Weiss, M.D

16 Clues to Your Past Lives, By Barbara Lane Ph.D

The Dream Book, By Betty Bethards,

The Desire Factor, By Christy Whitman

Now & Then, By Jacqueline Sheehan

Kitchen Table Tarot, By Melissa Genova,

It"s a Wonderful

Afterlife By Richard Martini

Loyalty to Your Soul By Ron and Mary Hulnick Ph.D

The Seat of the Soul. By Gary Zukav

The Magic of Intuition. By Florence Scovel Shinn

The Miracle Minute. By Mary Morriessey

Reincarnation and

Your Past-Life Memories. By Gloria Chadwick

ACKNOWLEDGMENTS

My sincere thanks to my husband Val and my daughter Lisa for their ongoing support;

I am thankful to my friends Bhumika Modi-Shupla and Jami Opyan, who knew about my desire to write the book from its very inception and patiently listened to my stories, sharing with me their genuine feedback.

My appreciation goes to Allison Armstrong, my writing coach, whose encouragement and guidance allowed me to expand my creativity and build trust in myself.

I am grateful to Lana Kirtser, my long-time friend, for the wealth of information she always was willing to share with me.

A special thanks to Grammarly because using this App was imperative for the timely completion of this book.

For over twenty-five years, many different Teachers were placed on my path to prepare me for the next steps of my evolution. I am deeply grateful to and for all who provided an environment for learning, inspiration, and upliftment; who taught me invaluable tools and unique skills; who opened my mind and heart to many possibilities and allowed me to learn from the best and grow into who I am today.

These are just a few to name here:

George and Alex Kappas from HMI, who taught me about the human psyche and human behavior;

Ron and Mary Hulnick Ph.D. from USM, who introduced me to the principles and practices of Spiritual Psychology,

Maria Nemetz from ACE, who taught me to see everyone through Green Lenses;

Joey Hubbard from the Insight Seminars, who taught me the Wisdom of the Soul;

Judy Nelson from the Clearsight Institute, who helped me to develop and nourish my metaphysical abilities;

Christy Whitman and Christina Hill from Christy Whitman International, The Council, and Athella for their inspiration, infinite wisdom, genuine support, desire to make a difference, and the invaluable skills like channeling and energy healing they taught me.

Mary Morrissey and everyone from the Brave Thinking Institute taught me how to create a vision and become a Brave Thinker.

Brian Weiss, MD, for his profound and revolutionary books that opened my eyes to the world beyond 3D, became an inspiration and a guiding star for my book.

Hay House for being a constant presence in my life for many years; their teachings, programs, and workshops allowed me to learn, grow, and become.

Steve Harrison for his incredible teachings, his generosity, and his heartfelt intention to be of service.

Bob Proctor for his life-long teachings, his motivation to inspire others to live an abundant life, his altruism, and his purposefulness.

And so many more teachers who made a long-lasting effect on me and whose teachings laid a foundation for my spiritual evolution and development.

I want to express my gratitude to all people who over the years encouraged, advised, prompted, and insisted on me writing a book. I heard you, and this book is a testament to your trust in my abilities and your genuine support.

Printed in the United States
by Baker & Taylor Publisher Services